Good Housekeeping

BOOK OF
GARDENING

Good Housekeeping

BOOK OF
GARDENING

EXPERT ADVICE AND TECHNIQUES FOR GARDENERS

COLLINS & BROWN

First published in the United Kingdom in 2011 by
Collins & Brown
10 Southcombe Street
London
W14 0RA

An imprint of Anova Books Company Ltd

The Good Housekeeping website is
www.allboutyou.com/goodhousekeeping

10 9 8 7 6 5 4 3 2 1

ISBN 978-1-84340-582-5

A catalogue record for this book is available from
the British Library.

Reproduction by Dot Gradations Ltd, UK
Printed and bound by Times, Malaysia

This book can be ordered direct from the publisher at
www.anovabooks.com

The following pictures are reproduced with the kind permission
of GAP picture library and Maxine Adcock, BBC Magazines Ltd,
Pernile Bergdahl, Dave Bevan, Richard Bloom, Christina Bollen, Elke
Borkowski, Julia Boulton, Jonathan Buckley, Keith Burdett, Leigh
Clapp, Sarah Cuttle, Paul Debois, Ron Evans, FhF Greenmedia,
Victoria Firmston, Tim Gainey, John Glover, Marcus Harpur, Jerry
Harpur, Neil Holmes, Mike Howes, Martin Hughes-Jones, Dianna
Jazwinski, Lynn Keddie, Geoff Kidd, Fiona Lea, Gerald Majumdar,
Fiona McLeod, Zara Napier, Clive Nichols, Brian North, Vic and
Julie Pigula, Howard Rice, S&O, JS Sira, Friedrich Strauss, Graham
Strong, Visions, Juliette Wade, Mel Watson, Rob Whitworth, Jo
Whitworth and Dave Zubraski: 2, 10(L), 11(T,B), 12, 18, 19(B),
20, 25(R), 28, 35, 48, 49, 52-53, 56, 67, 69(R), 70(L), 71, 73,
74(L), 75, 76, 80, 86(L,R), 87, 88(R), 93, 99(L), 101, 106(L,R),
109(L), 111, 118, 119, 120, 121, 122, 123, 124, 125(L,R),
130, 130, 133, 149, 152, 153, 162, 165(L), 169, 171(L),
177, 183, 185, 204(L,R), 208(L), 211(R), 221, 232, 237,
239(R), 240(L), 242 and 243(L).

Line illustrations by Trina Dalziel: 47 and 57.

Colour photography by Lucinda Symons: 15, 16, 17, 19(T), 21, 22,
23, 24, 25(L), 27 and 51.

The Publisher would like to thank Ginkgo Gardens for the kind use of
their centre.

Contents

Basics

Tools and materials

Before you get started on your garden you are going to need a basic set of tools. Always buy the best you can afford. Saving money on tools is a false economy. Choose those made from stainless steel with solid wood handles. Never buy unseen; try them out for size and comfort first.

It will make a big difference to your workload if your tools are comfortable to use. Take good care of them, as well. Clean off mud and soil after use and wipe them over with a cloth before putting them away. Service them regularly and sharpen them as necessary and they will last you for years.

Basic set

Spade: An essential tool, needed for heavy digging, breaking up clods and moving soil. They come in many different sizes and shapes, which is why you need to try them to find the one that suits you best. Make sure that the tread on the shoulders fits your foot comfortably, as well.

Fork: Used for loosening soil and breaking it down, especially after digging, and for lifting plants. The prongs are either round or flat – although if you are buying only one fork, the latter may be more useful as they do the minimum of damage to tubers when lifting plants.

Rake: Used for levelling soil, preparing seedbeds, and removing stones and debris. Widths vary, but an 8- to 10-tooth rake is adequate for most purposes. It is very important to make sure the weight and balance are right for you, as it is difficult to work with one that is too heavy or cumbersome.

Hoe: You will need two types: the Dutch hoe, which has a flat rectangular blade that is used, as you walk backwards, to remove weeds, loosen soil or draw a drill; and the draw or swan-necked hoe, which has a blade at right angles to the handle. This is pulled towards you rather than pushed away, and is useful on heavier soils.

Hand trowel and fork: The trowel is a versatile tool, but is primarily used for planting. The fork is useful for weeding near plants and loosening soil. They need to be sturdy and well made. They come in different shapes and sizes, so take your time to find the one that is most comfortable for you.

Garden line: Essential for making sure your rows are straight when planting seeds. You can buy it, or make your own by tying twine to two short canes.

Cultivator: Not essential, but the three to five claw-like prongs are useful for breaking up ground and weeding between plants.

Mattock: This is a heavy chisel-bladed hoe, again not essential, but sometimes easier to use on hard ground.

Pocket knife: Invaluable for slitting open bags of compost or manure, cutting twine, taking cuttings, etc.

Sharpening stone: Useful to have to keep edges sharp and well maintained.

Secateurs/shears: For pruning, cutting, and keeping things tidy.

Others

Watering can: Choose a sturdy one – plastic or metal – with a capacity of 7–9 litres (1½–2 gallons). You will need two detachable roses – one coarse and one fine – so you can match flow to plant.

Wheelbarrow: For moving large amounts of soil, manure, plants, bags, etc. Again, size and balance are personal and you may find a second-hand one does the job just as well.

Bucket: For holding soil and liquid materials, or moving quantities of stuff around the plot.

Carrying sheet or bag: Keep nearby while working to

Hand tools
Good-quality hand tools with solid wood handles make gardening much easier and last longer.

save time on trips to the compost heap or shed.
Bamboo canes: A selection of various sizes for marking out areas or positions, and providing support for plants, nets and wire.
Twine: For tying up branches, stems, canes, wires, etc.
Gloves: Choose a lighter, supple pair for pruning and planting, and a heavy-duty pair for messier jobs, such as handling prickly and stinging plants.
Horticultural fleece: To protect plants from the cold or pests, or to warm up the ground.
Cloches: A variety of different shapes, sizes and materials, including glass, plastic and polyurethane. For covering rows or individual plants – useful if you want to bring forward or extend the growing season, or for warming up the soil prior to sowing or planting.
Cold frames: Used for bringing on young plants or protecting a growing crop. They can be static with a solid floor, or movable (without a floor) to offer protection for plants growing in the ground, or adapted to make a hot bed.

For sowing seeds
Seed trays and small pots: Made of plastic (though wooden and terracotta types are also available) and used for sowing seeds that need to be pricked out when they have germinated.
Modules: For sowing individual seeds to grow on to the planting out stage.
Biodegradable pots: Used for sowing crops that do not like their roots disturbed. Once the seedling is large enough to be planted out in the ground, the whole container can go in and it will rot down as the plant grows.
Dibber: A pointed metal or wooden tool used to make holes for planting seeds or young plants. A small one is used for pricking out seedlings.
Labels and markers: Essential so you know what is where. Many different types are available in plastic, wood or slate with appropriate pencil or pen.
Propagator lids: Usually made of clear plastic and put over seed trays to speed up germination. You could also use cut-off plastic bottles set over individual pots.
Electric propagator: A small unit in which seeds are placed when a specific temperature is needed to germinate them (usually 13–16°C/55–61°F). The heat source may be a light bulb, heated plates or coils. Not essential, but a useful piece of equipment to have and they are usually inexpensive to run.

Choosing plants

Harmony is perhaps the most important word when it comes to making a garden. You want somewhere that is relaxing but also stimulating to the senses, in which art and nature have reached a happy equilibrium. Creating a balance between the different elements of a garden, such as the paving, lawn, trees, shrubs and flowers, is crucial to the end result.

Creating a structure

It is the larger or more upright plants that do most to develop the garden framework, dividing it into sections and serving as a guide as you walk or look around. Trees or shrubs with a narrow, vertical, columnar habit have lots of impact, and are useful as they take up little space. Trees, under whose branches you can walk, hedges that act as green walls, or plants with strong shapes all provide the visual 'bones' for the garden. The softer, more formless shrubs and flowering perennials are the 'flesh'. Some of the most successful gardens are those that balance the formality of clearly designed shapes, such as clipped hedges and topiary, with the informality of burgeoning borders of flowers and shrubs.

Year-round interest

Some gardeners are happy to have most of their garden flowering at once. They like to see a spring garden with lots of bulbs, or an early-summer garden with roses and perennials, and they are content to let it rest for the remainder of the year. Most gardeners, though, prefer to attempt a long season of interest, which involves trying to interweave plants so that there is always something, or some part, that looks good.

A garden takes time to develop, and never stands still. Planning planting for the short, medium and long term helps to avoid the great gaps that can try the patience of even the most dedicated.

Spring colour
An unusual, contrasting bedding design with magenta tulips and yellow wallflowers brings strong colour to the garden in spring.

Autumn foliage
A dramatic canopy of foliage can provide both colour and interest in the garden, as the contrasting golds of this *Liquidambar orientalis* and (behind) the reds of Japanese maple (*Acer palmatum* 'Osakazuki') demonstrate.

PLANTS FOR SPECIFIC CONDITIONS

When you are creating your garden and planning your plantings, it is important to analyse the different conditions in various areas, and then select and install suitable plants accordingly. What will grow well in full sun will not work in deep shade, and so on. Choose and buy your plants carefully.

Plants for dry sun
Many flowers like dry, sunny conditions. Tall purple alliums rise above pink aquilegias in this summer border.

Plants for shade
Many plants, such as euphorbia, thrive in shade or partial shade.

What grows best?

Before you select plants for your garden it is advisable to learn as much as you can about the area in which you live, since this will determine what you can grow. A good way of finding out which plants will grow well is to visit local arboretums and gardens that are open to the public.

Keep a notebook handy to record plants that you like and that thrive in gardens with similar conditions to yours. It is a good way of building up your own body of knowledge. Once you have a clear idea of what the area can or cannot offer, you will be in a position to select plants that will succeed with little effort on your part.

A wall or hedge that protects the garden from the prevailing wind may mean you are able to grow a range of more tender plants than anyone else in your neighbourhood. On the other hand, being in an exposed position, or in a frost hollow, where cold, heavy air gathers, can mean the opposite. Light is yet another very important factor. Is your garden shaded by trees, or is it on the sunless side of a hill or your house? If it is, then you need to concentrate your efforts on growing shade-tolerant plants.

The soil is the other major consideration. Is it generally damp or even wet, or is it very free-draining and so liable to dry out in summer? Is it fertile and is it acidic or alkaline? You may not require a soil-testing kit to find out – gardening neighbours can often supply the answers.

Hardiness rating

The hardier the plant, the lower the temperature that it will tolerate. In the following plant directory pages plants that will not survive temperatures less than 5°C (41°F) are described as 'tender' – meaning they are not at all hardy – in individual entries. Other plants are hardier, and are given ratings as follows:
* Half-hardy: will survive 4 to -1°C (30–40°F)
** will survive -1 to -7°C (20–30°F)
*** will survive -7 to -17°C (0–20°F)
**** will survive -17 to -30°C (-20–0°F)

The temperatures given in the individual entries denote the optimum growing temperature range for the plant in question.

Buying plants

To grow plants successfully it is important to start with a good, healthy specimen and to plant it correctly. Always buy your plants from a good garden centre or, better still, from a specialist nursery where you can obtain expert information and advice. Never be tempted to buy cheap plants in poor condition.

Check the plants over thoroughly and avoid any that are limp and drooping, with sparse stems and just a few pale or discoloured leaves. Look closely for any signs of disease or insect infestation and make sure that the soil has not dried out and shrunk away from the sides of the pot. If there is a mat of roots protruding from the base, this is a sign that the plant is rootbound and should have been repotted long ago. Having chosen a healthy specimen, take it home carefully. Carry it upright at all times and protect it from the risk of pieces breaking off. Do not leave it in a hot, airless vehicle for any length of time. When you arrive home, take it outside straightaway and water it thoroughly before planting as soon as possible.

To summarise, here are some top tips for buying fresh plants:

- Decide what type to purchase. It is important to read up on what types grow in your area, soil and climate.
- Check your local farm shop or fresh produce market, which often sells healthy plants that have not experienced the trauma of transportation.
- Check your local garden centre if you can't find a farm shop or if you want more exotic plants or a larger variety.
- Make sure the plants you choose are healthy. The leaves should be strong, shiny, green, and not browning, yellowing, wilting or mushy.
- Buy proper soil or mulch for the plants, along with transplanting containers. It is important to know which grow best next to each other to conserve as much room as possible.

Healthy roots
Tip the plant out of its pot before you buy it. Look for roots that reach out to the edges of the pot and hold the compost together; however, they should not wind round the inside of the pot or be growing out of the base of the container. The roots should look fresh and white, not brown or yellow.

BUYING PLANTS

When selecting plants, look for healthy, disease-free top-growth, a good overall shape, and small roots just emerging through the base of the container. They should not be too large with lush growth, as this indicates a soft plant that will not establish well. Plants should be well labelled with both the common and the Latin name, their eventual height and spread, their flower colours, and the type of site and soil required.

Stunted growth
This marjoram has been in the pot too long, resulting in stunted, woody growth on top and old roots coming through the pot base.

Poor root system
This plant is not ready for sale. It has only recently been potted and has little root system.

A well-grown plant
This well-grown marjoram has fresh, healthy top growth and no large roots growing out of the pot base.

Large root system
The large root system appearing from the pot base indicates that this rosemary should have been planted before now; the top is beginning to die off, indicating stress.

Poor shape
Avoid plants like this rosemary, which has a poor shape, is very spindly, and will not grow into a good specimen.

A healthy plant
An excellent specimen. It has good top growth and shape, and a few small roots just coming through the base.

Preparing the site

When you dig, you are creating better growing conditions for your plants. Digging opens up the soil and lets in air, which allows organic matter to break down more easily and release nutrients. It also improves drainage and encourages plants to form deeper root systems. As you dig, you have the opportunity to add manure or compost to the soil and to remove perennial weeds, or to bury annual weeds and other plant debris. All will add nutrients to the soil.

As a general rule, autumn is the best time to dig, especially when you are clearing a patch of land or beginning cultivation for the first time. At this time of year the soil should be perfect for preparation, neither too wet nor too hard. Leave the soil roughly dug over the winter months, so that the frost and rain can break down the larger clods of earth and improve the soil texture. Never dig the ground when it is frozen or waterlogged, because this severely damages the soil structure.

There are three different digging techniques. In simple digging (see opposite) a spadeful of soil is lifted and inverted as it is dropped back into its original position. In single digging the soil is cultivated to the depth of one spade, using a trench system, and in double digging the soil is cultivated to the depth of two spades, again working across a plot that has been divided into trenches. All have different purposes and have evolved over centuries.

Simple digging

This is the easiest and quickest method for garden digging, good for clearing shallow-rooted weeds and creating a fine layer of soil on the surface. It is useful when digging in confined spaces and around mature, established plants.

No trench system is involved in this form of digging. Just lift a spadeful of soil and turn it over before dropping it back into its original position. Then break up the soil with the spade, in a brisk, chopping action. When the ground has been thoroughly dug over, leave it for at least three weeks before any

planting or seed sowing is carried out. This will allow the soil plenty of time to settle and should be long enough for any buried weeds to be killed. The surface of the soil will begin to disintegrate and separate into smaller clods as it is broken down by the various actions of the weather. This will make it much easier to create a fine tilth on the surface later on, with the aid of a fork and a garden rake.

Using a fork

If the soil is particularly heavy and difficult to penetrate with a spade, it may be easier to use a fork, because the soil does not stick to the prongs in the same way that it does to a blade. Fork tines are ideal for breaking down the soil to a finer tilth, and teasing out unwanted plant roots and debris. However, in normal conditions, a spade is better for slicing through the soil and cutting through weeds.

The correct method

Many people dig incorrectly, with the doubly displeasing results that the soil is not properly cultivated and they risk back injury.

It is essential to adopt the correct posture and to use tools that are the right size and comfortable.

In the winter, make sure you are suitably dressed in warm clothes, since cold muscles are prone to injury. Do not dig too hard or for too long on the first occasion, and plan the order of work.

IMPROVING SOIL

While we cannot completely change the basic soil type we have in the garden and must learn to live with it to a degree, we can temporarily alter its pH (by adding lime), feed it and improve its structure. The aim is to end up with soil rich in humus with a top layer of fine, crumbly tilth. Even if your soil is naturally neutral and fertile, it will need a certain amount of organic material in order to remain so. While plants may grow happily in this type of soil in the first year, they will suck the nutrients out of it. The soil must be constantly replenished if you want to carry on getting a good harvest.

1 Organic compost made from organic garden waste is an invaluable source of nutrients. Check that the compost is well rotted before you put it on the ground, as fresh compost will burn any plants it comes into contact with.

2 Spread a thick layer of well-rotted organic matter onto the soil surface. Use a spade or fork to remove the compost from the wheelbarrow and then rake it evenly all over the area to be cultivated.

3 Dig the bed thoroughly with a garden fork, incorporating the compost and working it into the soil beneath the surface. The final bed should have a slightly domed surface, ready to receive the plants.

4 The bed is now ready for planting. Carefully remove the plants from their pots. Use a hand trowel to dig a hole to the depth of the rootball and place the plant in it. Backfill the hole and gently firm soil around the base of the plant.

Sowing seeds

Growing new plants from seed is the most common, and possibly the easiest, method of propagating a large number of plants quickly. It is ideal for growing plants for bedding displays and containers, and for filling gaps in summer borders.

INDOOR SOWING

Because some plants have tiny seeds and germination can take many weeks, even months in some cases, it is not always practical to sow in situ. Vermin or birds may take the seed; more usually, weed growth overtakes the sowing area, and distinguishing between weed and garden plant seedlings can be difficult. It is often best to germinate small seeds in controlled conditions indoors, in a seed tray rather than in the open ground.

1 Prepare the seed tray with special seed and sowing compost, levelling it off 0.6 cm (¼in) below the rim. Water with a fine rose until moist throughout.

2 Pour the seeds into the palm of your hand, pick some up between your thumb and forefinger, and sprinkle thinly and evenly over the surface of the seed tray. Do not sow too thickly.

3 Lightly cover with fine seed compost sieved through a plastic pot or sieve. Cover larger seeds to their own thickness or press them into the seed compost. Tiny seeds germinate best uncovered. Water gently with a fine rose.

4 Cover the seed tray with a sheet of glass or a plastic lid. This keeps moisture in, helps to eliminate the need for further watering, and prevents pests attacking the seeds and emerging seedlings. Keep in the shade.

DIRECT SOWING

Many plants can be sown directly into the ground where they are to grow. However, to achieve success and to have as many seeds germinate as possible, you must first ensure that the timing and conditions are just right. So the temperature must be suitable – most seeds will not germinate unless the average temperature during the day is above 6°C (43°F) – the soil must be well prepared and you must follow the seed company's guidelines as to planting depth and distance. In order for the seeds to germinate the earth must be warm enough and neither too dry nor too wet.

1 Prepare a seedbed by clearing any existing weeds, making a reasonably fine bed without too many soil lumps or stones.

2 Mark out different areas for the plants to go using sand. Even vegetable plants don't have to be grown in rows; a prettier arrangement might be more suitable for a garden setting.

3 Sprinkle seeds over the soil. Dust-like seeds should be scattered on the surface. Larger seeds should be pressed into the soil, to the same depth as the seed size. Sow sparsely to avoid having to thin out the seedlings.

4 If the seeds need to be covered (see step 3), use your fingers or a small fork to work them lightly into the soil. Firm the soil down gently and water with a fine rose.

Planting techniques

Plants that you have raised in the greenhouse or in an outdoor nursery bed, and those you have purchased from seed companies and the local garden centre, will eventually need to be planted out in their flowering positions. This needs to be done with a great amount of care, as the correct planting technique makes all the difference to subsequent growth and flowering. Poorly planted specimens may never become properly established and will fail to perform well.

Hardening off

Young plants that have been raised and grown on in a heated greenhouse, such as summer bedding plants, including all plug plants and larger young plants, must be gradually acclimatised to outdoor conditions before they are planted out, otherwise they will receive a severe check to growth. This technique, known as hardening off, is carried out in a cold frame.

Hardening off needs to start at least three weeks before planting out. Remember that frost-tender plants must not be planted out until danger of frost is over. If you don't have a cold frame, harden off young plants by taking them outside for longer and longer periods, before finally leaving them out overnight.

After putting the young plants in the cold frame, give a little ventilation for the first few days by opening the covers slightly during the day. Close the frame at night. Then over the next few weeks open the frame daily, gradually increasing the ventilation over this period by opening the covers more widely until fully open. But again, close the frame at night. A few days before planting out, the covers are left fully open at night also, provided there is no risk of frost.

It's important to keep an eye on your plants during the daytime as, if the cold frame is in direct sun, the temperature inside the small area can get very high, even in early spring. Young plants are very susceptible to drying out and wilting, even in a few hours.

Cold frames
Cold frames are smaller than greenhouses, aren't heated and can vary from large, brick-built structures to small, movable ones. They are a halfway house before the plants are put in the ground and are designed to keep the worst of the night cold or any frost off plants.

PLANTING

Fork over the top 15cm (6in) of soil, breaking down any lumps and removing all weeds. Add compost as a general soil conditioner. Thoroughly water the plant in its container well before planting, or if it is bare-rooted, soak the roots for approximately 15 minutes in a bucket.

1 Dig a hole slightly larger than the container. Loosen the soil at the bottom of the hole; if dry, pour water into the hole and allow it to soak away. Remove the plant from the pot and place it in the hole.

2 Return the soil around the plant and firm down with your hands. Water the plant to consolidate the soil around its roots. Water regularly until established.

Acclimatising plants
Young plants need to get used to the cold outside before they are put in the ground. If you don't have a cold frame, put them outside during the day but bring them under cover in a cool place, such as a garage, at night.

Propagation

It is both satisfying and economical to create beautiful displays in the garden by growing new plants from seeds and cuttings, or by dividing old, established clumps to form young, healthy plants. Many methods of propagation are very simple, once certain principles are grasped, and they require little equipment. When you have gained some experience, a simple plant propagator and a cold frame will allow you to grow wonderful summer bedding displays and a much wider range of plants than is available in the garden centre. An added bonus is that you can easily swap plants with friends.

What is propagation?

Propagation is the term used to describe the processes by which seeds or other parts of living plants are managed in order to produce more plants. This process can be carried out in two ways – by seed or vegetatively.

Seed is a sexual method of reproduction in which the seed develops following the fertilisation of the female part of the plant by male pollen. Vegetative propagation is an asexual method, which includes taking cuttings of stem or leaf, dividing rootstock, layering or grafting in order to produce more plants.

Sowing seeds (see pages 16–17) is the easiest and most reliable method of producing large numbers of plants quickly. Plants grown from seed are also, generally speaking, healthier and more disease-resistant.

Some plants, however, do not produce viable seed. The seeds may take a long time to reach flowering age, or do not breed true, which means that the seedlings can differ greatly from the parent plant in form, habit and flower colour. One advantage is that this variation allows many new and improved plants to be produced. However, in cases where an exact replica of the parent plant is desired – for example, in the propagation of especially fine forms of plants or of variegated plants – a vegetative method of propagation is used. This is the only way to be sure that any plant produced is identical in all its features to the parent plant.

Young cosmos plants
Growing new plants from seed is an easy, and inexpensive, way to increase plant stocks.

Choosing suitable plant material

Always choose cuttings or collect seed from the strongest and healthiest plants available to give the best possible chance of successful propagation.

Choose the best-formed fruits or seed heads and be aware that timing is critical when collecting seed. If you leave it too late, the seed will already have been dispersed, and if you gather seeds too early, they will not germinate. Gather seed on a dry day and if there is any dampness, put them in the sun to dry thoroughly. If you are not sowing them immediately, store them in a cool, dry place out of direct sunlight. If you are buying seed, select packets that are undamaged and that have the most recent date stamp, because old seed does not germinate so well.

Growing from cuttings

Increasing plants by taking cuttings from the stems is a common way to propagate woody plants. Stem cuttings are divided into three main types, according to the maturity of the plant and the time of year that the cuttings are taken.

Softwood cuttings are taken from shoots of the current season's growth as soon as a shoot's base starts to become firm, from late spring until late autumn.

Semi-ripe cuttings are taken from shoots of the current season's growth just as soon as the base of a shoot has turned woody, in late summer and autumn.

Hardwood cuttings are taken from fully mature shoots of the current season's growth of deciduous shrubs, trees and vines. They are cut from the parent plant immediately after their leaves have fallen, in late autumn and early winter.

Softwood cuttings

There should be minimal delay between removing a softwood cutting from the parent plant and potting it up, because immature stems are very prone to wilting.

Select a vigorous shoot on the parent plant and cut it 8–10cm (3–4in) long, with a sharp knife. Keep softwood cuttings in a closed plastic bag in the shade until you are ready to pot them up. Prepare each cutting by trimming the base and stripping away the lower leaves.

Dip just the base in rooting hormone powder and tap the cutting to shake off any excess. Insert at least 5cm (2in) of the stem into a soilless cutting compost. Water the pot thoroughly, ideally with sterilised water, preferably containing a fungicide. To prevent wilting, softwood cuttings should be kept in a well-lit, enclosed, damp environment while they grow roots.

1 Lift the plant and remove complete sections of root.

2 Cut the end of the root nearest to the plant straight across.

3 Cut the thinner end, nearest to the root tip, with a sloping cut.

4 Insert cuttings so the straight end is level with the mix.

HOW TO DIVIDE ROOTS

Propagating from pieces of root is a good technique for certain hardy perennials, including those that do not lend themselves to division. Plants that are often propagated from root cuttings include acanthus, globe thistle (*echinops*), Japanese anemones, mulleins (*verbascum*), oriental poppies (*Papaver orientale* cultivars), pasque flower (*pulsatilla*), border phlox, drumstick primrose (*Primula denticulata*) and sea holly (*eryngium*).

5 Cover with moist sand to stop the cuttings drying out.

21

Semi-ripe cuttings

Semi-ripe cuttings are propagated in a similar way to softwood cuttings, but at a later time of year. The stems of semi-ripe cuttings are therefore harder and more resilient than softwood cuttings. Potting up quickly is not quite so critical, because the cuttings will not wilt as quickly as softwood cuttings. Semi-ripe cuttings do, however, take longer to grow roots and there are various techniques that are adopted to improve rooting. Unlike softwood cuttings, any soft, sappy growth should be removed from the tip of a semi-ripe cutting before it is inserted into the cutting compost. Cuttings should be placed in a plant propagator or other closed environment while they produce roots. Semi-ripe cuttings, taken in autumn, can be left to root slowly over winter in a cold frame.

Hardwood cuttings

Hardwood cuttings can be taken at any time in late autumn and winter, but those taken before the cutting is fully dormant, in late autumn, are likely to be the most successful. They are planted outdoors and because the soil is moist and relatively warm, they have a chance to produce small roots before the onset of winter and should start into stem growth by mid-spring. Select a healthy shoot, 23–60cm (9–24in) long, from the current season's growth of the parent plant. Cut it straight across the bottom of the stem with sharp hand pruners. Cut the tip at an angle (but if the buds are arranged opposite each other, as in buddlejia, make a straight cut).

In a well-cultivated part of the garden, make a series of holes for the cuttings by pushing the tines of a garden fork 15cm (6in) into the soil. Insert one cutting into each hole so that it presses into the bottom. At least two-thirds of the cutting should be in the ground. Rake the soil around the cuttings and press it firmly around them. If conditions are dry, finish by watering the soil well. Then leave the cuttings to grow.

Division

You can increase most perennials by splitting a clump of plants, complete with roots and growth buds, into small sections, each of which grows into a new plant, identical to the parent. Either plant the divisions straight into their new site or into spare ground until they are ready to be planted out permanently. You can rejuvenate many perennials in this way every three to four years. Division is best carried out when plants are semi-dormant and the soil is workable. Early spring is the main season.

Plants with fleshy roots, such as hostas, need to be cut with a sharp knife into sections, ensuring that each has its own roots and growth buds. Carefully cut away and discard any old and rotten portions of the roots. Replant divisions immediately in well-prepared soil, and water them with a fungicidal solution to prevent them rotting. Plants with fibrous roots can be divided by easing the roots apart with your fingers or a knife. If the roots are too tough, you can split them into manageable sections with a garden fork. Replant immediately after division.

HOW TO DIVIDE PLANTS

Depending on the size and toughness of the plant, there are various methods that can be used to divide roots. Care should always be taken to be as gentle as possible so that minimum damage is caused.

1 Prise apart soft and fleshy roots using your fingers.

2 Tougher roots may require the use of a sharp knife.

3 Use a garden fork on bigger plants with tough roots.

CLEANING AND STORING SEEDS

If seeds are to be collected and stored for use next season, they need to be reasonably free of debris. Many seed heads, such as those of lavender below, are cut on their stems and are ready for cleaning.

It is most important to make sure that the seed is absolutely dry before storing.

Warning Asthma sufferers and those sensitive to dust should not clean seed. For others a simple face mask can be worn to protect from dust.

1 Remove the dried heads from the stems. Pick out any stems, leaves and larger pieces of debris.

2 Rub the seed heads to make sure all the seeds have come out and then sieve through a fine mesh to clean the seed further.

3 Gently blowing the seeds will remove any remaining dust. The seeds are now ready for packing in a bag or envelope.

4 Label with the common name, the Latin name and the date, and store in a cool, dark, dry place.

23

Watering

Water is essential for all plant growth, although some plants have adapted to drought conditions and need very little moisture in order to survive. If you live in a climate with low rainfall, it is important to choose plants that will tolerate dry conditions, unless you are able to spend time and thought on watering systems. Roof gardens and other sites exposed to drying winds increase the watering needs of your plants.

A variety of watering systems and devices are available to help you in your gardening, notably drip-watering systems and water-retaining granules. It is best to water at dawn or dusk when the sun's rays are less powerful and the evaporation rate is much reduced. To encourage deep roots to develop, water thoroughly and regularly rather than little and often.

Easy-watering systems

In any garden easy access to water is essential, as many plants will require regular watering. An outdoor tap is vital, unless the kitchen tap is easily accessible. Also essential is a hose that is long enough to reach the farthest corners of the garden.

In times of drought, however, water may be rationed and you may well have to recycle washing water from the house. Installing a water barrel to collect runoff rainwater is a sensible precaution.

There are some simple systems available which deliver water to the garden, as needed, at the flick of a switch. If you have a small garden in a warm climate, or if you garden on an exposed site, such as a roof terrace, consider planning a soaker hose or drip-feed system, which can be laid permanently in the planting areas.

Drip-feed system

This consists of a series of fine-bore pipes, with drip heads at intervals, that you can position exactly where water is required – at the foot of plants needing

HOW TO WATER CONTAINERS

Plants in containers lose water very rapidly through evaporation. Terracotta pots especially are notoriously poor at retaining moisture. Hanging baskets, with their small amount of soil and large area exposed to the elements, are very greedy for water and may well need watering once a day in hot weather. Group containers together to preserve moisture, and put them in shade in hot weather.

Watering the root base
To make sure water penetrates the potting compost thoroughly, make a few holes around the edge of the pot with a cane before watering.

frequent watering, for example. A soil-moisture detector can be fitted to the system, ensuring that the automatic system is overridden if the ground is sufficiently damp. Drip-feed systems tend to get blocked with debris, so it is important to clean the system regularly.

Leaky-pipe hose system
This is useful for watering large areas, such as lawns, or for planted beds. It is an efficient way of using water, because it is directed straight at the roots. The hose is punctured with a series of fine holes so that a regular, even supply of water is delivered over the length of the hose. A similar system uses a porous hose. The system can be buried beneath the soil to make it both permanent and unobtrusive.

Retaining moisture
A major difficulty with growing plants in containers is keeping the plants supplied with water, especially when using soilless potting composts, because these are very difficult to rewet after drying out. To overcome this, add granules of polymer to the mix. When wetted, these granules swell to form a moisture-retaining gel that can hold vast amounts of water. The water is gradually released into the mix.

Making the most of water
There are various ways to reduce the need for watering. Firstly, you need to increase the moisture-retaining properties of the soil, if it is sandy, by adding plenty of organic matter. Secondly, you need to reduce the amount of water lost through evaporation, by screening your plants from the effects of drying winds.

If your flowers are in containers, grouping plants together helps to reduce evaporation, as does using pebbles or stones over the soil surface.

Drought-resistant plants
If you live in a very dry climate with free-draining soil, you need to make sure your plants are as drought-resistant as possible, to give them the best chance of success. This will save you from spending a great deal of time watering. Generally speaking, apart from those succulent plants which store water in their tissue (either in their leaves or stem), plants that are tolerant of drought can be recognised by their foliage. It is usually silver-grey, finely divided, and sometimes covered in fine hairs or felt – all of which reduce evaporation.

Reviving a wilting plant
If a plant is wilting from lack of water, plunge it into a bowl of water so that the pot is covered. Leave it until air bubbles subside.

Watering hanging baskets
Hanging baskets dry out very quickly. Always soak the basket so the water runs out from the bottom and all the compost is wet.

25

Feeding

In order to grow well, plants need a balanced diet of nutrients. Nitrogen, phosphorus and potassium are the foods plants must have in large amounts to sustain a good growth rate. Nitrogen is needed for healthy growth and leaves, phosphorus is essential for good root development, and potassium ensures both healthy flowers and fruits as well as disease resistance.

As a gardener, you should supply your plants with these nutrients in various forms, depending on the circumstances. Some forms are particularly useful for conditioning the soil, others for supplying a direct source of food to the plant itself. Quantities of nutrients required depend on how intensively the garden is cultivated: closely packed vegetables require a great deal; shrub borders much less. Fertilisers contain plant nutrients in a concentrated form and are used in fairly small quantities. Manures are bulky and need to be added to the soil in large amounts – but they provide only a small quantity of nutrients. However, they do add valuable fibre, which is converted into humus to condition the soil. This also increases the activity of beneficial micro-organisms.

Composting animal manure
Animal manure is one of the best soil conditioners because it improves soil texture and provides some nutrients, while the straw provides bulk. Compost manure for at least six months before adding it to the soil.

Fertilisers

These may be organic or inorganic in their origin. Organic fertilisers consist of dead plant or animal matter that has been processed, such as bone meal, dried blood and fishmeal. They do not scorch foliage and are natural products. Inorganic fertilisers, also known as artificial, chemical or synthetic fertilisers, are derived from mineral deposits or manufactured by an industrial process. These are highly concentrated and faster-acting than organic types, but you must not exceed the dosage, or plants may be scorched or damaged.

Fertilisers can be applied in dried form or dissolved in water, as in liquid fertiliser.

Soil conditioners

Digging in quantities of bulky, organic matter introduces both nutrients and fibre into a garden soil.

Woody and fibrous material opens up heavy soils and improves the soil structure. It provides materials that improve moisture retention on lighter soils. Fibrous conditioners of this kind are ideal if long-term soil improvement is the ultimate aim. When they decompose, they contribute to the formation of humus, which absorbs other nutrients applied to the soil. Lime, while not a food, is also used to condition the soil. Never apply lime to the soil at the same time as fertilisers and manures.

Green manure

Organic matter can be added to the soil by growing a fast-maturing crop as temporary ground cover on a

APPLYING LIQUID FERTILISERS

Liquid is usually easier and safer to apply than dry fertiliser, and the plant's response is often more rapid. The concentrated fertiliser is diluted in water. It is applied either to the soil or to the leaves, depending on the type. Mix the fertiliser thoroughly with the water before application, to reduce the chance of damaging the plants. Do not apply when rain is forecast, or it may be washed through the soil away from the plant's roots.

1 Dilute liquid fertilisers with water and apply with a watering can or a hose. These fast-acting fertilisers are useful for correcting nutritional deficiencies.

2 Apply liquid fertilisers as a foliar fertiliser or directly to the soil around the base of a plant. Most foliar fertilisers are soil-acting as well so runoff is absorbed by the roots.

bed that is empty for a while, usually over the winter. The crop is dug into the topsoil six to eight weeks after germinating. This fast-maturing crop is known as a green manure and it is a means of improving both organic matter and nitrogen levels. The release of nitrogen is quite swift and so provides an early boost to plant growth. The greener and younger the manure, the less fibre is produced.

Dry fertilisers

These are nutrients in a dry, solid form – granules and pellets. They are mixed together and coated with a wax or resin compound that slowly dissolves and releases fertilisers into the soil. The release can take 6–18 months, depending on the thickness of the outer coating, soil moisture, temperature and pH. Apply these fertilisers by sprinkling them evenly over the soil and mixing them into the top layer with a fork. If the soil is dry, water the area after application to dissolve the fertiliser and wash it down to the root zone. An even distribution of fertiliser is essential, because damage to plants may occur if too much is used. Mark out the area you intend to fertilise into squares with canes and garden lines, and then take care to sprinkle and spread the fertiliser as evenly as possible.

Fertilising container-grown plants

To promote balanced and healthy growth in containers, use brand-name potting composts that contain measured amounts of fertiliser.

Additional fertilisers can be given if necessary by applying quick-acting fertilisers as a top-dressing, or by using foliar fertiliser or fertiliser spikes.

Mulching

A weed is any plant growing in a place where it is not wanted. Many weeds cause problems just because they are so tough and versatile that they can adapt to a wide range of growing conditions. For this reason they must always be dealt with before they get out of control. The most effective way to prevent them appearing in the first place is to use a mulch.

Mulching for weed control

Mulching is the practice of covering the soil around plants with a layer of material to block out the light and help trap moisture. In today's gardens, where plastics are commonplace, inorganic (non-biodegradable) black plastic sheeting is often chosen. Although not inviting to look at, it can be hidden beneath a thin layer of more attractive organic (natural and biodegradable) mulch.

As a general rule, organic mulches provide the bonus of improving the fertility of the soil, but inorganic mulches are more effective because they form a better weed barrier. To be fully effective as a barrier, organic mulches must be applied as a layer at least 10cm (4in) thick. Both organic and inorganic mulches tend to be less effective against established perennial weeds, unless an entire area can be sealed until the weeds have died out and planting is carried out through the mulch while it is in place. One way of clearing weedy ground in summer is to cover the soil with a mulch of clear or white plastic, sealed around the edges. Weeds are gradually killed by a combination of high temperatures and lack of carbon dioxide.

The plastic sheeting can be removed after a time and used elsewhere. The treated area is weed-free, ready to plant and cover with an organic mulch, such as shredded bark or gravel (see below).

Gravel mulch
Covering the soil with a mulch such as gravel will block out light and prevent weed seeds germinating.

Types of weeds

Weeds compete directly with your garden plants for light, nutrients and water. They can also act as hosts to pests and diseases (see pages 32–3), which can spread as the season progresses. Groundsel, for instance, often harbours the fungal diseases rust and mildew, and sap-sucking aphids. Chickweed also plays host to aphids as well as red spider mites.

Perennial weeds

Digging up perennial weeds is an effective disposal system, provided that most of the root system is removed from the soil. If only a few weeds are present, try digging them out with a knife or trowel, but you must remove at least the top 5cm (2in) of root close to the surface to prevent the weed regrowing. This method can be used in the lawn to get rid of individual or small patches of weeds, and is a reliable means of eradicating weeds growing close to garden plants. In this situation, often no other weed control method would be effective without risking damage to plants growing nearby.

Clearing weeds

The simplest way to deal with weeds is to remove them physically, either by pulling or digging them out or, if they are small, hoeing them off at soil level.

The biggest problem with this method of control is that most weed seeds require exposure to light before they germinate. Often, when weeding disturbs the soil, more air is allowed into the surface layers and an ideal seedbed is created. Although the existing weed seedlings are destroyed, the weed growth cycle starts all over again. This problem is often worse when using rotovators, because they leave the surface layers of soil light and fluffy, making a perfect seedbed. Perennial weeds are increased, too, because they are chopped into pieces, each capable of growing.

The most effective way to clear weeds, especially established perennials, is to use a combination of

cultural and chemical methods. Spray weeds in full growth with a chemical herbicide and, as they start to die, bury them when the area is dug over. When the new weed seedlings germinate, spray them with a chemical while they are most vulnerable.

Annual weeds

Clearing annual weeds with a hoe is quick and effective, but the timing is important. The hoeing must be done when the weeds are tiny and before they start producing seed.

Hoeing will sever the stems of young weeds from the root system just below soil level. This both prevents the stem forming new roots and stops the roots producing a new stem. When hoeing, make sure you always walk backwards to avoid treading weeds back into the soil.

There is an old saying, 'One year's seeds make seven years' weeds', which has now been endorsed by scientific research and proved to be remarkably accurate – unfortunately for gardeners.

Annual weeds are capable of producing a staggering total of 60,000 viable seeds per square metre per year. The vast majority of these seeds are found in the uppermost 5cm (2in) of soil, but they will usually germinate only when exposed to sufficient light levels. This is why mulching (see opposite page), which covers the soil and blocks out light, has become such a widely popular method of weed control. The added benefit of mulching is that there is little chance of contaminating the soil with chemical residue.

General care

With some additional care, various plants can be made to flower longer, some tender kinds can be kept for a number of years, and hardy varieties can be encouraged to remain young and vigorous. It will also ensure that borders and beds remain neat and tidy at all times.

Dead-heading

The removal of dead flower heads helps to ensure a neat and tidy appearance, and also encourages some plants to flower for a longer period. This applies especially to annuals and tender perennials, but also to some hardy perennials – for example, delphiniums and lupins may well produce a second flush of flowers later in the summer if dead blooms are removed.

Dead flower heads are usually cut off with some of the flower stem attached, using secateurs or flower scissors. With others, such as marigolds (*tagetes*) and pelargoniums, the dead blooms are easily snapped off between finger and thumb, thus speeding up the process. You may be able to use garden shears for plants that produce masses of very small flowers.

Remember that the dead flower heads of some hardy perennials look attractive over winter and can therefore be left until they become tatty in early spring. Examples are the flat-headed stonecrops (sedums) and achilleas, and ornamental grasses, including miscanthus.

Over-wintering plants

Many tender plants used for summer bedding or containers can be kept from year to year, by rescuing them before or when the frosts start in autumn. For example, tender perennials such as pelargoniums, fuchsias and osteospermums can be propagated from cuttings in late summer or early autumn and the resultant young plants wintered in a cool but frost-free greenhouse. The parent plants are lifted and discarded as they will probably be too big to store under glass and in any case young plants are best for replanting. Tender winter-dormant tubers, such as dahlias, cannas and tuberous begonias, are lifted, cut down and stored in boxes of peat substitute in a cool, frost-free place over winter.

Annuals, whether tender or hardy, are pulled up and discarded when frosts start in autumn, as they cannot be kept from year to year, although you may be able to save the seeds for sowing in spring.

Renovating borders

Borders or beds devoted to hardy perennials, or parts of the borders where perennials are grown, need renovating every three to four years. This allows for improvement of the soil by digging and manuring, and if necessary the removal of any perennial weeds that have become established.

Border renovation also enables plants to be rejuvenated. The plants are lifted and heeled in on a spare piece of ground while the border is being dug. Then the large clumps of plants are split or divided into smaller portions, using the younger, more vigorous parts around the outside edge for replanting. The older centre part, which is declining in vigour, is discarded.

Borders and beds can be dug in the autumn and the plants split and replanted in early spring of the following year, or the whole operation can be undertaken in early spring if that is more convenient.

Supporting plants

Fortunately, the majority of perennials and other plants are self-supporting, but there are some with weak or thin stems, or with heavy flowers, that will need artificial supports to stop them being flattened by wind and rain. Climbing plants, such as honeysuckle or passionflower, must also have supports.

Thin- or weak-stemmed hardy perennials, especially if they are tall, such as some cultivars of Michaelmas daisy (*aster*) and bellflower (*campanula*), can be supported with twiggy hazel or birch sticks pushed in around and among them as they are starting into growth. Tall multi-stemmed annuals can be supported in the same way. Alternatively, metal plant supports which link together around the plant, forming the size required, are very effective.

Single bamboo canes can be used for tall annuals with single stems, such as sunflowers (*helianthus*). Heavy plants, such as dahlias, are best supported with a single wooden stake, about 2.5cm (1in) square, with each stem tied to it as it grows. Support each stem of a delphinium with a single bamboo cane.

Make sure all supports are shorter than the flowering height of the plants and tie in stems loosely with soft garden string.

Climbing annuals, such as sweet peas, can be grown up a wigwam formed of bamboo canes. Alternatively, use an obelisk. Various kinds are available, including smart metal versions or more rustic ones made from willow or hazel. Some are suitable for patio tubs. Climbers can be supported on walls or fences with trellis panels fixed to the structure. Annual climbers can also be grown through larger plants such as shrubs.

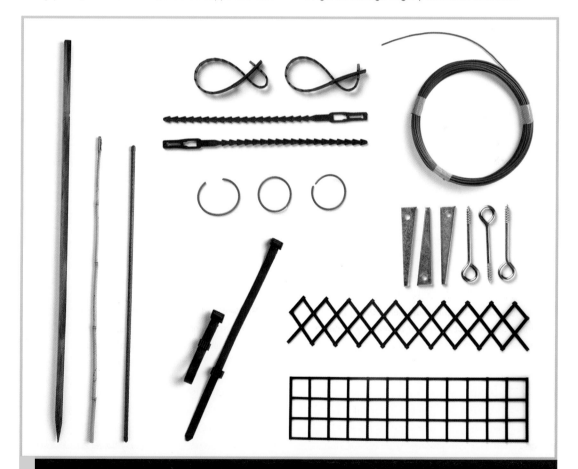

Types of support
Most flowers do not require support, but some taller perennials with weak stems or large, heavy flowers will benefit from staking or other support with anything from a bamboo cane to an obelisk made of willow.

Pests and diseases

These are the major pests, diseases and other problems that affect flowers. However, do not be alarmed, as although there are numerous things to be concerned about, your plants are unlikely to be troubled by all of these. For proven environmental reasons, there is a strong emphasis in these pages on non-chemical methods of control of the pests and diseases discussed.

Aphids

These are among the most troublesome of insect pests, particularly greenfly and blackfly, and they attack a wide range of flowers. Wash off aphids with plain or soapy water, or spray with insecticidal soap if necessary.

Black root rot

A disease affecting many flowers. The roots become black, but above-ground symptoms are yellowing and wilting leaves. Scrap sickly looking plants and plant something different in the affected site.

Bulb and corm rot

Bulbs of various kinds, including daffodils, lilies and tulips, are prone to rotting in store, caused by various diseases. Check for soft spots, particularly at the base of the bulbs (basal rot). Remove and discard rotting bulbs. Similarly, corms such as crocuses and gladioli are prone to several kinds of rot while in store, so check regularly and remove and discard any that show signs of rot.

Bulb aphids

Certain aphids winter on bulbs and corms in store. Look out for them on crocuses, gladioli, lilies and tulips especially, and simply rub them off.

Caterpillars

The caterpillars of various moths and butterflies eat holes in the leaves of numerous perennials and annuals. They are generally green, brown or grey and are usually hairy. Caterpillars are easily picked off

and destroyed, or plants can be sprayed with an insecticide if necessary.

Cutworms

These caterpillars, the larvae of several different moths and greenish brown or greyish brown in colour, live in the soil and feed on roots and stem bases of plants, causing young plants to wilt and die. Remove any found during soil cultivations.

Damping off

This disease affects seedlings indoors, causing them to collapse suddenly and die. Damping off can spread rapidly and should be prevented by using sterilised compost and clean containers.

Earwigs

These night-feeding insects, easily recognised by their rear pincers, eat holes in flowers, buds and leaves. Remove and destroy them. Spray plants with an insecticide if necessary.

Foot rot

This disease causes the bases of stems to turn black and rot. Pull up and discard any plants that show signs of infection.

Grey mould

This major fungal disease, also known as botrytis, can infect all top growth of plants – flowers, buds, leaves and stems – resulting in rotting. Cut off any affected parts of plants, back to healthy tissue.

Leaf spot

Many diseases show up as brown or black spots on the leaves of numerous ornamental plants. The spots vary in size and some are in the form of rings. The best control method is to pick off any leaves showing spots. Spray affected plants with fungicide if necessary.

Mildew

The most common is powdery mildew, appearing as white powdery patches on the leaves of many plants. Remove affected leaves. Spray plants with fungicide if necessary.

Petal blight

This disease attacks chrysanthemums, and sometimes other related plants, and anemones, showing as watery lesions or brown spots on the petals. Remove affected flowers. Spray plants with fungicide if necessary.

Red spider mite

There are several kinds of these microscopic spider-like creatures that feed by sucking the sap from the leaves of many plants, particularly under glass. This results in fine, pale yellow mottling on the upper leaf surfaces. Spraying plants regularly with plain water will deter the mites, or spray plants with insecticidal soap if necessary.

Rhizome rot

This bacterial disease causes the leaves of rhizomatous irises to turn yellow and wither. Dig up and discard badly affected plants. Avoid damaging surrounding plants as you do this.

Rust

This fungal disease shows as rust-coloured, orange, yellow or dark brown raised spots on the leaves and stems. Affected leaves should be removed. Spray with a fungicide if necessary.

Slugs and snails

Slugs and snails eat the leaves of a wide range of plants and also damage soft young stems and even flowers. Control by placing slug pellets around plants. Alternatively, remove them by hand.

Stem rot

Numerous diseases, but particularly sclerotinia, cause the stems of various perennials and annuals to rot. As there is no cure, plants that are badly affected should be removed and discarded.

Tuber rot

A fungal disease may attack dahlias in store, causing the tubers to rot. Check stored tubers regularly and if rotting is noticed, cut it away to healthy tissue.

Viruses

Viruses are types of diseases that infect a wide range of plants. The most common symptoms are stunted and distorted plants. There is no cure: pull up and burn affected plants.

Weevils

These beetles are easily recognised by their elongated 'snout'. Their larvae are the main problem. Their feeding causes wilting, and invariably death in severe attacks. Use biological control with a pathogenic nematode in late summer.

Wilting leaves

Apart from wilting caused by various pests and diseases, the most common cause is drought. Young plants may never recover, even if watering is carried out. Make sure the soil never dries out, ideally by mulching permanent plants and by watering as necessary.

Woodlice

These pests feed at night and hide in dark places during the day. Physical control is not practical, except to ensure that any plant debris is not left lying around.

Designing your vegetable plot

Many people grow vegetables only if they can find some spare room in the garden, while for others the challenge is to produce a year-round supply of home-grown food. The planning and layout of a vegetable plot, and the types of vegetable chosen, will be influenced by the number of people who want to eat home-grown vegetables, and the vegetables they like the most.

It should be possible to keep a family of three supplied with vegetables year-round from a plot measuring around 7 x 4m (23 x 13ft), but a good supply of produce can actually be grown on an area much smaller than this. Where space is limited, greater yields can be produced by plants that grow vertically rather than those that spread sideways.

Choosing a suitable site

The ideal site on which to grow vegetables is one that is warm and sunny during the growing season, and has plenty of light and good air circulation, while being sheltered from strong winds (since wind exposure can reduce plant growth by up to 30 per cent). The air flow is particularly important for wind-pollinated crops, such as sweetcorn, and to reduce the incidence of pests and diseases, which is worse in still air conditions. A gently sloping, sunny site is perfect for an early start in spring, because it will warm up slightly quicker than other aspects. On steeper slopes, plant across the slope rather than down it, because this will reduce soil erosion during heavy rain.

Planning the vegetable plot

An efficient vegetable garden should be planned to make the best use of sun, shelter and space. The vegetables should be planted in rotation groups (see pages 40–41) to ensure pests do not build up.

It is important that you organise your vegetable plot as efficiently as possible to ensure that the crops are rotated correctly and that you make the maximum use of the available sun and shelter.

Plant the tallest crops (such as Jerusalem artichokes or scarlet runners) so that they do not block the light from the smaller-growing vegetables. Use the walls or fences for shelter, and for supports for beans, peas or cordon or espalier fruit trees.

Remember to leave yourself ample space to walk between the blocks or rows of vegetables. Trampling on the soil will destroy its structure and reduce its potential yield.

Growing in containers

Vegetables, fruit and herbs can all be grown in containers in the most unlikely of places – on patios, balconies and walkways, or on any small plot of ground where the light is good. You can even grow some vegetables on your windowsill!

Although you will naturally want to choose the most attractive container for your vegetables, for successful results the container's appearance is not nearly as important as the contents. Whatever the plant to go in it, you need to fill the container with fresh, well-balanced potting mix and a base dressing of fertiliser, adding further top-dressings of fertiliser throughout the growing season. Long-rooted vegetables, such as carrots and parsnips, require deep containers (at least 45cm/18in deep) in order to grow satisfactorily.

Tall crops tend to become unstable, especially if grown in small pots, and can blow over in strong winds, so protect these with stones or netting. Container-grown crops need to be watered frequently during warm or dry weather.

Planning an attractive vegetable plot
Growing edible crops can be as satisfying visually as it is in culinary terms, as this elegant
vegetable plot demonstrates.

A year in the vegetable plot

EARLY SPRING

GENERAL TASKS

- Prepare seedbeds and cover with cloches or black polythene to warm up.
- Check beds are ready for the new season's crops and all weeds and roots have been removed.
- Feed overwintered crops with a general fertiliser or mulch.
- Keep an eye on weeds and watch out for early signs of pests. Cover vulnerable plants with netting or fleece.
- Order seeds and young plants from mail-order companies.
- Check stored vegetables regularly and get rid of any that show signs of deterioration.
- This is the start of the busy season for sowing seeds, pricking out and potting on – check there is plenty of space in cold frames as well as the greenhouse and shed.

TIME TO SOW

In situ: American land cress, beetroot, broad beans, carrots, chicory (heading), kohlrabi, peas (earlies), radishes, rocket, spinach, spring onions, turnips.

In a nursery bed: Brussels sprouts (earlies), cabbage (autumn and winter), globe artichokes, leeks, lettuce.

Under glass: Aubergines, broccoli (calabrese), cauliflowers (summer), celery, chard, okra, onions, peppers, pumpkins, shallots, squashes, tomatoes (indoor).

TIME TO PLANT/TRANSPLANT

In situ: Asparagus, cabbage (summer), cauliflower (summer), garlic, globe artichokes, Jerusalem artichokes, onions, potatoes (earlies), shallots.

Under glass: Salad leaves (earlies), tomatoes.

IN SEASON

American land cress, broccoli (sprouting), Brussels sprouts, cabbages, cauliflowers, celeriac, celery (trench), chard, chicory (forced), lamb's lettuce, leeks, lettuces, parsnips, pumpkins, radishes, rhubarb (forced), spinach, spring onions, swedes, turnip tops.

LATE SPRING

GENERAL TASKS

- Begin to move young plants outside to start the hardening-off process.
- Keep an eye on the soil and water if it becomes very dry. Mulch when the soil is moist to help retain water.
- Hoe regularly to keep on top of weeds and check for signs of pests and disease – especially under cloches or fleece.
- Stay on top of thinning out, earthing up potatoes and providing support for climbers such as peas and beans.
- Clear beds of overwintered vegetables. Store remaining crops and add stumps, roots and any that are not good enough to keep to the compost heap.
- Prepare beds for new crops: put in supports for netting or wire cages; erect cane supports as required; dig a trench for celery; and prepare planting holes for cucurbits.

TIME TO SOW

In situ: American land cress, asparagus, beetroot, broad beans, broccoli (calabrese), carrots, chard, chicory (heading and forced), endive, fennel, kale, kohlrabi, lettuce, onions (bulbing and spring), parsnips, peas, radishes, rocket, spinach, swedes, turnips.

In a nursery bed: Broccoli (sprouting), Brussels sprouts, cabbages (autumn and winter), cauliflowers (autumn and winter), kale, leeks.

Under glass: Beans (borlotti, French and runner), cardoon, courgettes, cucumbers, pumpkins, squashes, sweetcorn, tomatoes (outdoor).

TIME TO PLANT/TRANSPLANT
In situ: Asparagus, brassicas (earlies), cabbage (summer), globe artichokes, Jerusalem artichokes, onions, potatoes.

Once all danger of frosts has passed: Aubergines, beans (borlotti, French and runner), celeriac, celery, peas (earlies), peppers, sweetcorn, tomatoes (outdoor).

Under glass: Aubergines, cucumbers, tomatoes.

IN SEASON
American land cress, asparagus, broad beans, broccoli (sprouting), Brussels sprouts, cabbages, carrots, cauliflowers, chard, kale, leeks, lettuce, radishes, rhubarb, salad onions, spinach, turnip tops, turnips.

EARLY SUMMER

GENERAL TASKS
- Sow intercrops such as lettuces where there is space. Lightly fork over the ground and add fertiliser first.
- Apply a general fertiliser or high-potash feed to plants that need it, such as squashes, cucumbers and tomatoes.
- Watch for pests and take precautions. Keep on top of watering and weeding.
- Stake, tie in and train side shoots on crops such as beans, cucumbers and tomatoes.
- Order in any seedlings or young plants needed for autumn and winter sowings.
- Start harvesting crops as they are ready.
- It's easy to forget at this time of year to continue with successive sowing to provide a continuous supply of

crops. Sow seeds in situ, or under cover for transplanting later.

TIME TO SOW
In situ: American land cress, beetroot, cardoon, carrots, chard, chicory (heading and forced), courgettes, endive (frisée), fennel, kale, kohlrabi, lettuces, peas, radishes, salad onions, spinach, squashes, swedes, sweetcorn, turnips.

In a nursery bed: Brassicas (winter).

TIME TO PLANT/TRANSPLANT
In situ: Beans (borlotti, French and runner), brassicas (autumn and winter), celery, cucumbers, globe artichokes, leeks, lettuces, okra, peppers, pumpkins, squashes, sweetcorn, tomatoes.

IN SEASON
American land cress, asparagus, broad beans, broccoli (calabrese), cabbages, carrots, cauliflowers, chard, endive, kohlrabi, lamb's lettuce, lettuce, onions (salad and overwintered bulbs), peas, potatoes, radishes, rhubarb, spinach, turnips.

LATE SUMMER

GENERAL TASKS
- Keep picking repeat-producing crops such as beans, courgettes and tomatoes to encourage more to grow.
- Clear away crops that have finished and dig over the ground to expose any pests or weeds in the soil.
- Pests and diseases spread quickly in hot, dry weather, so stay vigilant. If it's wet and humid, watch for potato blight, which thrives in those conditions.
- If you have suitable space, plant up a green manure crop.
- Clear cold frames and the greenhouse ready for sowing and growing winter crops that need protection from frosts.
- Weed, mulch and water.

TIME TO SOW

In situ: American land cress, beetroot, carrots, chard, chicory (heading), Chinese cabbage, endive (broad-leaved), fennel, kohlrabi, lamb's lettuce, lettuce, mizuna greens, onions (bulbing and salad), pak choi, peas (autumn), radishes (summer and winter), spinach (winter), turnips.

In a nursery bed: Cabbage (spring and red varieties), kale.

TIME TO PLANT/TRANSPLANT

In situ: Broccoli (sprouting), cabbages (spring), cauliflowers (autumn and winter), kale, leeks.

IN SEASON

American land cress, aubergines, beetroot, borlotti beans, broad beans, broccoli (calabrese), cabbage, carrots, cauliflowers, celery, chard, cucumbers, endive, French beans, garlic, globe artichokes, kohlrabi, lamb's lettuce, leeks, lettuce, onions (bulbing), potatoes, radishes, runner beans, salad onions, shallots, spinach, squashes, sweetcorn, tomatoes, turnips.

EARLY AUTUMN

GENERAL TASKS

- Cover late and overwintering crops with cloches or fleeces if the weather turns cold.
- Clear spent crops and supports from beds ready for autumn digging and liming.
- Cover root vegetables that are being left in the ground with straw, or lift and store in a frost-free place.
- Start gathering together used pots, seed trays, labels, canes, etc., and clean and store ready for future use.

TIME TO SOW

In situ: Broad beans, carrots, peas, rocket, spinach (winter).

In a nursery bed: Cabbages (spring), cauliflowers (summer).

Under glass: Lettuces, mizuna greens, pak choi, radishes.

TIME TO PLANT/TRANSPLANT

In situ: Cabbages (spring), garlic, onions (autumn).

Under glass: Lettuces.

IN SEASON

Aubergines, beetroot, broccoli (calabrese and sprouting), Brussels sprouts, cabbages, cardoons, carrots, cauliflowers, celeriac, celery, chicory (heading), cucumbers, endive, fennel, French beans, Jerusalem artichokes, kale, kohlrabi, leeks, lettuces, mizuna greens, okra, onions, pak choi, parsnips, peas, peppers, potatoes, pumpkins, radishes, runner beans, spinach, squashes, swedes, sweetcorn, tomatoes, turnips.

LATE AUTUMN

GENERAL TASKS

- Clear all non-hardy crops and dig over the ground. If it's heavy, leave clods on top to allow the frost to break it down.
- Lift and store any remaining winter crops that are at risk of severe weather. Check any stored crops are still in good condition.
- Earth up stems of cabbages, cauliflowers and Brussels sprouts to protect from windrock.
- Gather leaves together to make your own nutritious leaf mould to use as a mulch (it should be ready in a year). Erect a simple structure of wire netting wrapped around three or four stakes and pile in the leaves, pushing down firmly; or pack them into black

plastic bags, punch in a few holes and leave to rot down – this may take longer than a year.

TIME TO SOW
In situ: Broad beans, carrots, peas.

Under glass: Lettuces, mizuna greens, pak choi, radishes, rocket.

TIME TO PLANT/TRANSPLANT
In situ: Cabbages (spring), garlic, onions (autumn).

IN SEASON
American land cress, Brussels sprouts, cabbages, carrots, cauliflowers, celeriac, celery, chard, chicory (heading and forced), Chinese cabbage, endive, fennel, Jerusalem artichokes, kohlrabi, kale, lamb's lettuce, leeks, lettuce, mizuna greens, okra, pak choi, parsnips, potatoes, pumpkins, radishes, rhubarb, spinach, swedes, turnips.

WINTER

GENERAL TASKS
• Carry on with digging and preparing soil as weather permits.
• Continue to check stored crops regularly for signs of mould, pests or diseases.
• Clean cloches and cold frames that are not in use.
• If bad weather is forecast, lift a supply of fresh vegetables so that you do not need to do so in the snow or frost.
• Check compost bins: empty them out, mix the contents together, then refill.
• Put out cloches, cold frames, black polythene or straw to warm up beds ready for early plantings.
• Clean and sharpen tools for the start of the new gardening year. Check over equipment – including sundry items such as seed trays, canes, labels, string, etc. – replacing or supplementing where needed.
• On a fine day, walk around your plot to remind yourself of the year's successes and failures, making

notes if necessary, to help to plan next year's crops and rotations. Order in seeds and young plants.

TIME TO SOW
Under glass: Aubergine, beetroot, broad beans, cabbages (summer), carrots, cauliflowers (summer), celeriac, celery, cucumbers, leeks, lettuces, onions, radishes, salad onions, spinach.

TIME TO PLANT/TRANSPLANT
In situ: Garlic, globe artichokes, rhubarb, shallots.

IN SEASON
American land cress, broccoli (sprouting), Brussels sprouts, cabbages, carrots, cauliflowers, celeriac, celery, chicory (heading and forced), endive, fennel, Jerusalem artichokes, kale, kohlrabi, lamb's lettuce, leeks, lettuces, mizuna greens, pak choi, parsnips, radishes, rhubarb (forced), spinach, swedes.

Planting techniques

Vegetables tend to be relatively short-term crops, because most grow rapidly and are harvested before they reach maturity. There are various ways in which you can maximise the efficiency of your vegetable plot in order to achieve the best possible yield of a number of different crops at all times.

Planning to avoid a glut

Take care when planning your garden not to grow too many of one type of vegetable that will ripen all at the same time. Do not overestimate your requirements.

Try to time your planting to produce a staggered harvest. For example, in the summer you may wish to eat a lettuce only every other day – that is, seven in a fortnight; don't therefore plant a dozen F1 hybrids that will mature at the same time – instead, plant six and another six a fortnight later.

Some crops, particularly the short-term salad crops, are the most susceptible to gluts and gaps, but this can be avoided to a large extent by sowing batches of seed on a planned basis. Timing of sowings can be difficult to gauge, but a good guide is to choose the date when you hope to harvest the crop and count back from there the number of weeks needed for the plants to grow. Most of the information for this simple exercise will be given on the back of the seed packet.

To make the maximum use of the available soil, some vegetables, such as cabbages, cauliflowers and leeks, can be grown in a seedbed until they are large enough to transplant, and then they can be planted in their cropping area. This is a very helpful technique that can be introduced for a wide range of vegetables, and is invaluable for plants that would otherwise occupy the ground for a long period of time at a wide plant spacing.

The disadvantage of transplanting young plants is that the disruption may check their growth unless they are kept well watered so that they establish and grow quickly. This is particularly critical where the transplants are dug up from a seedbed and replanted; some roots will always be damaged by this process, and a good supply of water is essential to help these plants recover. If they are short of water, many vegetables will 'bolt' – that is, the plant will stop growing leaves and develop instead a flower-bearing stem in an attempt to produce seeds.

A timing guide to successional sowings is to make the next sowing when the previous sowing has germinated and emerged through the soil.

Crop rotation

When groups of related vegetables are grown on a different plot from year to year, this is called crop rotation. One reason for moving crops from one part of the plot to another is to avoid the build-up of diseases and pests in the soil. Another benefit is that the soil's fertility can be improved by growing crops that add nitrogen, such as peas and most beans. Start by making a list of the various vegetables you intend to grow and then classify them into groups, based on their needs in terms of space and growth patterns.

Allocate each rotation group to a plot of land and draw up a month-by-month cropping timetable. This will keep the land fully occupied and provide continuity. For example, after Brussels sprouts and leeks are finished in early spring, follow with sowings of peas, carrots, lettuces or bunching onions.

If you prefer, the vegetables can be from different crop groupings, which means that the rotation from one plot to another is a gradual process rather than a wholesale changeover on a certain date.

If there is not enough space in a small garden to rotate entire blocks of vegetable crops, you could grow the plants in narrow strips instead and then regularly swap the groups between the strips.

Grouping the different types of vegetables together makes crop management easier. Leave at least two years before planting any vegetable from the same group in the same ground.

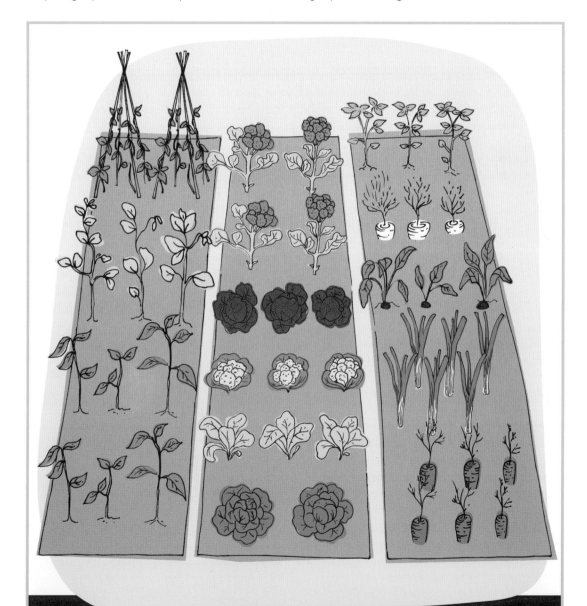

Crop rotation groups
This plot is divided into three groups: peas and beans (left), brassicas and leafy crops (middle), and roots and stems (right). A fourth, permanent, plot can be created for crops that are not shifted, such as asparagus. Each group is moved each year onto a new strip of land.

Harvesting, storing and freezing

When to harvest vegetables and how to store them will depend on a number of factors, including the time of year and the type of vegetable. Most vegetables are harvested when fully mature, but a few, such as spinach, can be cropped repeatedly as a cut-and-come-again crop.

Leafy vegetables, such as Brussels sprouts, are quite hardy and will survive outdoors in temperatures well below freezing point. Many root vegetables, however, have a high moisture content and are easily damaged in winter, even if left in the soil. Exceptions to this are carrots, parsnips and swedes, which are particularly hardy and can be allowed to overwinter in the ground until they are required for consumption.

The main causes of deterioration during storage are moisture loss from the plant tissue (with beetroots and carrots in particular drying out very quickly), or infection and rotting of damaged tissue caused by rough handling when the vegetables were being harvested. Onions and potatoes both tend to bruise particularly easily.

Some vegetables, such as onions, chilli peppers, peas, beans and garlic, will keep quite well if stored in a dry condition. If they are not to deteriorate, they must be allowed to dehydrate slowly in a cool, dry place. Once dry, beans and peas can be stored in airtight containers. Garlic, chilli peppers and onions can be hung up in an airy place. Any storage area must be frost-free.

Many vegetables also freeze well. These should be blanched before being cooled rapidly and frozen in sealed, airtight boxes or bags.

Ripe vegetables and fruit wait for no one. Always harvest your crops when they are ready and if they cannot be eaten straight away, dry them or freeze them for use later.

It is unlikely that the harvest from a container kitchen garden will be large enough to cause any major storage problems. However, that said, there is every reason to do what you can to ensure that nothing is wasted and that you are able to make the most of your harvest and enjoy all the fruit, vegetables and herbs that you have grown when you want to eat them.

Drying and storing

If you have enough space, then a number of vegetables, such as onions and potatoes, can be dried off and stored in a cool, dry, dark place for several weeks. Carrots and beetroots can also be stored in boxes of sand.

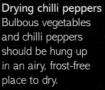

Drying chilli peppers
Bulbous vegetables and chilli peppers should be hung up in an airy, frost-free place to dry.

Harvesting parsnips
Parsnips can be left to overwinter in the soil and dug up as required.

Harvesting young vegetables
Always harvest young vegetables when they are fresh; many become overripe quickly. Freeze any surplus that you cannot use straight away.

	Crop rotation group	Ease of growing	pH range	Suitable for freezing	Length of growing season	Yield kg per m² (lb per yd²)	Tolerates frost
Asparagus	3	M	6.0–7.5	✓	52	1.8 (3.3)	✓
Asparagus peas	1	M	6.0–7.0	✗	7	1.2 (2.2)	✗
Aubergines	3	E	5.5–6.5	✓	9	6 (11)	✗
Beetroot	3	M	6.5–7.5	✓	8	2.4 (4.4)	✓
Broad beans	1	M	6.5–7.5	✓	20	4.8 (8.8)	✓
Broccoli	2	M	6.0–7.0	✓	8	2.4 (4.4)	✓
Brussels sprouts	2	E	6.0–7.5	✓	8	1.8 (3.3)	✓
Butter beans	1	E	6.5–7.0	✓	10	3 (5.5)	✗
Cabbages	2	E	6.5–7.5	✓	10	4.8 (8.8)	✓
Calabrese	2	E	6.5–7.5	✓	8	2.4 (4.4)	✗
Cardoons	3	D	6.5–7.5	✓	52	1.8 (3.3)	✓
Carrots	3	M	6.0–7.5	✓	8–12	2.4 (4.4)	✓
Cauliflowers	2	D	7.0–7.5	✓	8–10	5.4 (10)	✓
Celeriac	3	M	6.5–7.5	✓	14	3.6 (6.6)	✓
Celery	3	D	6.5–7.5	✓	14	4.8 (8.8)	✓
Chicory	2	D	6.5–7.5	✗	12	0.5 (0.9)	✓
Chilli peppers	3	M	5.5–6.5	✓	9	1.8 (3.3)	✗
Chinese cabbage	2	E	6.5–7.5	✓	8	1.8 (3.3)	✗
Courgettes and marrows	3	E	5.5–6.5	✓	8	2.4 (4.4)	✗
Cucumbers	3	E	5.5–6.5	✗	8	3.6 (6.6)	✗
Endive	2	M	6.5–7.5	✗	12	1.8 (3.3)	✓
Florence fennel	3	D	6.0–7.5	✗	12	3.6 (6.6)	✓
French beans	1	D	6.5–7.5	✗	8	2.4 (4.4)	✗
Garlic	3	M	6.5–7.5	✗	12	2.4 (4.4)	✓
Globe artichokes	3	D	6.5–7.5	✓	52	1.8 (3.3)	✓
Jerusalem artichokes	3	E	6.5–7.5	✗	52	3 (5.5)	✓
Kale	2	E	6.5–7.5	✓	10	1.8 (3.3)	✓
Kohlrabi	2	M	6.5–7.0	✓	6	3 (5.5)	✓
Lamb's lettuces	2	E	6.5–7.5	✗	8	1.2 (2.2)	✓
Leeks	3	M	6.5–7.5	✓	18–20	1.8 (3.3)	✓
Lettuces	2	E	6.5–7.5	✗	7	1.2 (2.2)	✗
Mangetouts	1	E	6.0–7.0	✗	12	1.8 (3.3)	✗

	Crop rotation group	Ease of growing	pH range	Suitable for freezing	Length of growing season	Yield (kg per m²/ lb per yd²)	Tolerates frost
Mizuna greens	2	E	6.5–7.5	✓	10	1.8 (3.3)	✗
Okra	1	E	6.5–7.0	✗	7	2.4 (4.4)	✗
Onions	3	M	6.5–7.5	✓	10–26	1.8 (3.3)	✗
Pak choi	2	E	6.5–7.5	✓	6	1.8 (3.3)	✗
Parsnips	3	M	6.5–7.5	✓	14	1.8 (3.3)	✓
Peas	1	E	6.0–7.0	✓	12	3.6 (6.6)	✗
Peppers	3	E	5.5–6.5	✓	9	1.8 (3.3)	✗
Potatoes	3	E	5.5–6.5	✓	14–22	3.6 (6.6)	✗
Pumpkins	3	E	5.5–6.5	✓	8	3.6 (6.6)	✗
Radishes	3	E	6.0–7.0	✗	3	0.5 (0.9)	✓
Rhubarb	3	E	6.5–7.5	✓	8	2.4 (4.5)	✗
Rocket	2	E	6.5–7.5	✗	10	0.6 (1.1)	✓
Salsify	3	M	6.5–7.5	✗	20	1.8 (3.3)	✓
Black salsify	3	M	6.5–7.5	✗	24	2.4 (4.4)	✓
Scarlet runners	1	E	6.5–7.5	✓	10	4.8 (8.8)	✗
Shallots	3	M	6.5–7.5	✓	10–26	1.8 (3.3)	✗
Sorrel	2	E	6.5–7.5	✗	10	0.6 (1.1)	✓
Spinach	2	E	6.5–7.5	✓	6	1.8 (3.3)	✓
Squashes	3	E	5.5–6.5	✗	8	2.4 (4.4)	✗
Swedes	3	E	6.0–7.0	✓	10	2.4 (4.4)	✓
Sweetcorn	3	E	6.0–7.0	✓	10	0.6 (1.1)	✗
Sweet peppers	3	M	5.5–6.5	✓	9	1.8 (3.3)	✗
Swiss chard	2	E	6.5–7.5	✗	9	1.2 (2.2)	✓
Tomatoes	3	E	5.5–6.5	✓	10	3 (5.5)	✗
Turnips	3	E	6.0–7.0	✓	6–10	1.8 (3.3)	✗

Crop rotation group = 1 Peas and beans, 2 Leaves and flower heads, 3 Roots, stems and fruiting vegetables

Ease of growing = D difficult, M moderate, E easy

pH range = preferred pH

Suitable for freezing = ✓ yes, ✗ no

Length of growing season = from outside planting (in weeks)

Yield = pounds per square yard

Tolerates frost = ✓ yes, ✗ no

Choosing pots and containers

The most important thing when choosing containers is to ensure that they fit in with their surroundings. Another is cost – handmade terracotta is expensive, but a search of junk or antique shops may produce worthwhile trophies for little money. Whatever style of pots you choose, make sure that they will look good together and will complement the overall style of your garden.

If you plan an extensive container garden, then you will need containers of various shapes and sizes for large and small plants. If they are to be grouped, then the groupings must match. One of the most popular materials is terracotta, with pots available in many shapes and sizes. Many of the designs are copies of Victorian styles which were available in the nineteenth century, and some of the more elaborate urns are based on classical designs. If you do not like the rather raw orange-brown colour of new cheap pots, you can tone them down by painting them in soft colours. Alternatively, encourage them to 'age' more quickly by painting them in yogurt or a mixture of sour milk and yogurt; this attracts algae, and within just a few weeks will give the pot a pleasant greenish patina.

Troughs and basins

A container garden which consisted of only pots would look rather dull and consequently it is worthwhile incorporating a number of troughs as well. The most expensive and heaviest of these are made from lead, but there are now many designs manufactured from fibreglass or stone. You could also use kitchen sinks.

Always position large pots, urns and troughs before filling and planting them; once full, they may be too heavy to move. Place the empty pots where you think you would like them to go, then move them around before you fill them up, trying out different arrangements until you are satisfied they fit the space and look good in your chosen locations.

Groupings of containers
They don't have to be all of the same material, but containers will look better together if you keep to the same look – either traditional or modern.

Most containers are made from terracotta, literally 'baked earth'. New pots can be painted or aged to look good in any area.

WHAT TO CHOOSE

There is a wide variety of containers available. Here are some tips to help you to choose what is best for you.

If you are clustering pots together, choose different sizes for as much variety as possible.

Look for frost-resistant labels on terracotta pots. These will withstand cold winters.

Terracotta pots come in lovely shapes, but choose a wider neck for greater plant accessibility.

Terracotta containers make great window boxes, but check them for fit before you buy.

A low, wide container is perfect for displaying low-growing plants such as sedums.

Reconstituted stone containers look very realistic and are a fraction of the cost of those made from carved stone.

Fake lead pots look very much like the real thing, but are much lighter and easier to handle. They are also a great deal less expensive to buy.

Hanging baskets

Hanging baskets are especially useful for placing on balconies or to cover walls or trellises. Once lined and planted, they can look most attractive. Planting hanging baskets is not nearly as difficult as it might appear. They should be planted in late spring, although they need protection overnight if there is any threat of frost.

Liner options

Traditional wire hanging baskets must be lined before use. Moss-lined baskets look spectacular, as the wire framework allows you to plant the sides and base of the basket as well as the top, but they drip when watered and dry out quickly. Modern, solid-sided hanging baskets are easier to look after, but you cannot plant the sides. For the best of both worlds, use one of the modern liners inside a traditional basket.

Solid baskets

Baskets with solid sides include plastic and self-watering types as well as plastic-lined wicker baskets, which now come in a range of novel shapes, including the cornucopia and cone. These are simple to plant up, although rarely as luxuriant as open-sided baskets, which allow a wider variety of plants to be used.

Large solid baskets do have the advantage of not drying out as quickly, especially ones containing a self-watering reservoir. These have a base covered with capillary matting below the compost and plants, and a wick that extends from that and dips into the reservoir. There are seep holes at the top of the reservoir so that excess water can drain away, and more sophisticated models usually have a watering tube which directs water straight into the compartment. If you follow the manufacturer's instructions, once a good root system has established, you should be able to leave the basket unattended for a couple of days.

A conical basket allows planting at the top but not in its sides.

A traditional basket like this is perfect for a reservoir. Even an old saucer placed inside the basket will capture some of the water and hold it for the plants.

For a full display like this, plants need to be positioned all around the sides of the basket as well as in the top of the compost.

Choosing the growing medium

There are three groups of compost and a number of special composts for different plants. For general container gardening, sowing seeds or planting, a good, multi-purpose compost is best.

Seed composts

Seed composts are specifically formulated for growing seeds. They may be loam-based (that is, contain soil) or be peat- or peat-substitute-based. They contain few nutrients; they are very fine so that the seed has close contact with the compost; and they retain water well. If seedlings are kept in seed compost for any length of time after germination and before pricking out, they will need additional feeding.

Multi-purpose composts

These can be used to germinate seedlings and also to pot up many plants. They fall in between seed and potting composts. If you are going to use multi-purpose for pots, then you will need to feed more than if you used a normal potting compost, but this is only a minor consideration. These are probably the best composts to buy for general garden work, but they should not be used for containers with large permanent plants.

Potting composts

Composts are either loam-based or peat-based. Loam-based composts are all based on the John Innes formulae. They retain water and nutrients better than peat-based composts and are more suitable for long-term growth. John Innes No. 3 contains three times more nutrients than John Innes No. 1 and is the best compost for established plants and trees.

Peat-based compost (including peat substitutes such as coir) is more readily available, lighter, cleaner and easier to work with. Use it for general gardening in smaller containers.

Special composts

A number of special potting composts are available, including ericaceous compost for acid-loving plants, orchid compost, alpine and cacti composts, bulb fibre compost, and hanging basket compost that contains water-retaining granules.

If you live in an area where the soil is very alkaline, you can grow acid-loving plants in containers rather than in your unsuitable garden soil. This applies more to flowers and shrubs, such as camellias and rhododendrons, than it does to fruit and vegetables, but some fruit must be grown in ericaceous compost.

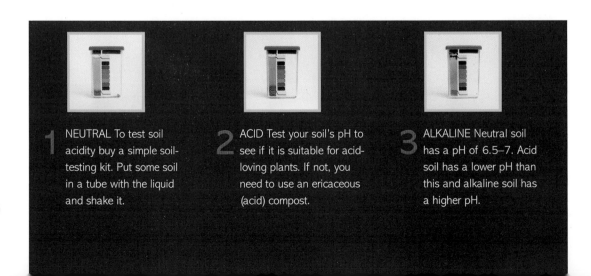

1 NEUTRAL To test soil acidity buy a simple soil-testing kit. Put some soil in a tube with the liquid and shake it.

2 ACID Test your soil's pH to see if it is suitable for acid-loving plants. If not, you need to use an ericaceous (acid) compost.

3 ALKALINE Neutral soil has a pH of 6.5–7. Acid soil has a lower pH than this and alkaline soil has a higher pH.

Potting and repotting plants

The principles of planting and repotting are the same. Plants need to be firm in the compost to prevent air pockets around their roots and have adequate drainage to avoid waterlogging.

POTTING A PLANT

It can take a lot of compost to fill a large, deep container, and if you plan to use only bedding plants, for example, that root into just the top layer, you may be wasting money. Fill the bottom third to a half of the pot with broken up polystyrene plant trays, old bricks or rubble. Pour on coarse gravel or chippings until the surface is levelled and cover with fine plastic mesh to prevent soil washing down between the cracks. This method also ensures excellent drainage. Alternatively, you could put a smaller pot inside the neck of the larger pot, hidden by the rim and if necessary supported on pebbles or gravel.

1 Add stones or broken crocks to the container to provide drainage.

2 Add compost to the bottom of the container so that the plant will sit a few centimetres below the rim of the pot.

3 The best way to remove the plant from its original pot is to squeeze it and gently tip it out. Do not pull it out, as you may damage it.

4 Add compost around the plant, pushing it down firmly with your fingers. Water the container thoroughly.

51

Growing herbs

Herbs – that is, plants that are valued for flavour, scent or some other qualities, which are used in cooking, as medicines, and for spiritual purposes – are fairly easy to please. Most of them grow vigorously in the wild and some may even be classed as wild flowers or weeds. The majority need little more than a sunny situation and a free-draining soil. However, as with all plants, it pays to find out which conditions your herbs prefer.

Choosing herbs

The herbs you choose to grow are very much a matter of personal taste, quite literally in the case of culinary herbs. In addition to those for the kitchen, and those for herbal remedies, a number attract benevolent insects, such as bees and butterflies, and you could just as easily make a herb garden for encouraging wildlife.

Herbs, like other garden plants, divide into those that have woody stems (shrubs and subshrubs such as lavender and rosemary), soft-stemmed perennials that come up year after year, such as lemon balm (*Melissa officinalis*) and horseradish (*Armoracia rusticana*), and annuals that are grown every year from seed, such as basil (*Ocimum basilicum*).

In a larger garden herbs can be grown in their own specific border or mixed with other plants in the perennial border. How you grow them, and even buy them, will depend on which group they belong to. Generally speaking, shrubby herbs can be grown from cuttings, while annuals are grown from seed.

Aromatic herbs

One of the most appealing aspects of many herbs is that they smell so good in the garden, especially when they are brushed against as you walk past them.

Siting aromatic herbs
Plant aromatic herbs in a prime position, such as either side of a path – brushing against the leaves
releases their scent.

A broad selection of aromatic herbs is listed on pages 188–99 of the plant directory.

Culinary herbs

Herbs for culinary purposes are used fresh or dried. Although dried herbs can be more pungent, when fresh they give dishes a delicious flavour, notably fresh basil with pasta, rosemary with grilled meat, and tarragon with chicken. By adding herbs to food, not only do you enhance flavour, but you also benefit from the important vitamins and minerals that these plants contain. As the types of food we eat have changed, influenced by factors such as health and convenience, and the popularity of exotic foods has grown, demand for more unusual herbs has increased. Many varieties, such as thyme, will keep very well in a dried form. However, to get the maximum benefit and the fullest flavour from herbs, they should be used fresh immediately after harvest. Plant culinary herbs close to the kitchen door to allow you to gather them while you cook. There is a broad selection of the most popular culinary herbs on pages 200–23 in the plant directory.

Medicinal herbs

For medicinal purposes, herbs can be infused or macerated. Herbal teas are made by infusing leaves in boiling water and letting it stand for a few minutes. Macerated herbs are left in oil for 10 days or so, until it becomes infused with the properties of the herb. Plants have been used for thousands of years to help to ease the symptoms of illness, long before chemical drugs became available. Indeed, many of the drugs which are now regarded as common – such as aspirin – had their origin in plants. Even a small garden will hold sufficient plants to make up a basic medical kit, and by drying and storing them, you will have medications to hand year-round. The herbs listed in the medicinal section of the plant directory

(see pages 224–51) are among the most popularly used for common complaints.

Warning Consult a herbal medicine expert before trying any treatments, since some herbs are toxic and/or have unwanted side effects, particularly in certain illnesses or conditions.

Ornamental herbs

Some herbs are grown primarily for their looks – and there are a large number that offer striking form and colour in the garden at all times of year. In this book these herbs have been classified as 'ornamental'. A selection of the best of these herbs is to be found on pages 251–2 in the plant directory.

Herbs for more difficult habitats

There are many well-known herbs that enjoy a site in full sunlight – such as lavender, thyme, rosemary and sage – but those that are suitable for more 'difficult' habitats in the garden, such as deep shade, partial shade and wetland areas, are not generally recognised to the same degree. The table opposite lists a number of species and varieties that will grow well in these less hospitable areas of the garden.

Buying herb plants

When selecting plants, look for healthy, disease-free top growth, a good overall shape, and small roots just emerging through the base of the container. They should not be too large with lush growth, as this indicates a soft plant that will not establish well. Always buy your plants from a good garden centre or, better still, from a specialist nursery where you can obtain expert information and advice. Never buy cheap herbs in poor condition. Plants should be well labelled with both the common and the Latin name, their eventual height and spread, their flower colours, and the type of site and soil required.

Most herbs prefer a sunny, open site, but here we list a selection of those that will tolerate other locations.

SUITABLE HERBS FOR A FULLY SHADED HABITAT

Aquilegia vulgaris
Columbine

Digitalis purpurea
Purple foxglove

Fragaria vesca
Wild strawberry

Galanthus nivalis
Snowdrop

Galium odoratum
Sweet woodruff

Gaultheria procumbens
Wintergreen

Geranium maculatum
Spotted cranesbill

Geranium robertianum
Herb Robert

Hyancinthoides non-scripta
Bluebell

Lysimachia nummularia
Creeping Jenny

Primula vulgaris
Primrose

Pulmonaria officinalis
Lungwort

Sambucus nigra
Elder

Scutellaria lateriflora
Skullcap

Trillium erectum
Birthroot

Vinca major
Greater periwinkle

Viola odorata
Sweet violet

SUITABLE HERBS FOR A PARTIALLY SHADED HABITAT

Achillea millefolium
Yarrow

Ajuga reptans
Bugle

Arctostaphylos uva-ursi
Bearberry

Chelidonium major
Greater celandine

Cimicifuga racemosa
Black cohosh

Clematis vitalba
Travellers' joy

Cytisus scoparius
Broom

Daphne mezereum
February daphne

Galanthus nivalis
Snowdrop

Gillenia trifoliata
Indian physic

Helleborus niger
Christmas rose

Hesperis matronalis
Sweet rocket

Humulus lupulus
Hop

Lilium martagon
Martagon lily

Lonicera periclymenum
Honeysuckle

Myrrhis odorata
Sweet cicely

Polemonium reptans
Greek valerian

Ranunculus ficaria
Lesser celandine

Rosa canina
Dog rose

SUITABLE HERBS FOR POND AND WETLAND HABITATS

Althaea officinalis
Marsh mallow

Angelica archangelica
Angelica

Caltha palustris
Marsh marigold

Cardamine pratensis
Lady's smock

Eupatorium purpureum
Joe-Pye weed

Filipendula ulmaria
Meadowsweet

Geum rivale
Water avens

Iris pseudacorus
Yellow flag

Iris verisolor
Blue flag

Lobelia cardinalis
Cardinal flower

Lobelia syphilitica
Great lobelia

Lysimachia vulgaris
Yellow loosestrife

Lythrum salicaria
Purple loosestrife

Mentha aquatica
Water mint

Mondara didyma
Bee balm

Nymphaea alba
White water lily

Succisa pratensis
Devil's-bit scabious

Valeriana officinalis
Valerian

Designing your herb garden

Herbs are so versatile that half the fun of growing a collection is designing the garden or feature they are to make. If you want just a few culinary species within easy reach of the back door, you can grow a selection of herbs in containers or in a bed alongside easy-to-grow vegetables. The informal herb garden may look slightly shaggy and a little bit wild, but in fact grows to quite a strict plan.

If you prefer a formal style, herbs are equally adaptable. Large leaves with well-defined shapes, such as acanthus, make strong statements. Small, finely cut or feathery leaves, such as those of fennel, produce softer and denser forms. Experiment with contrasting textures and colours.

Herbs have become increasingly popular for culinary purposes, and even for general medicinal use. They are extremely versatile, producing roots, stems, flowers, seeds and leaves that can have multiple uses, even when they come from the same plant. If you design the herb garden in an attractive, formal way, with the squares or segments divided into different families or species of herbs, it will make using the herbs much simpler. Herb gardens have been popular for centuries, and there is no shortage of information on how to design them, and the best herbs to grow for different purposes. Ideally, however, you should limit your ambitions to a few good, all-round culinary herbs, and some that have medicinal uses. Do not be tempted into practising with complicated home remedies: leave it to the experts, because some herbs are extremely powerful and could endanger your health.

Planning your herb garden

Careful advance planning is always worthwhile before you begin to plant your garden. Keep in mind how you plan to use the garden and how it will look in winter. Sketch a plan of your garden with any new and existing features. Use books, magazines and other gardens for additional inspiration; the planting suggestions in this chapter are also good starting points. Refer to the plant directory on pages 186–252 to help you to plot heights, spreads, colours and so on. Make sure that the garden works as a whole, each area merging with the next. Select plants for each season so that your garden contains flowers and foliage year-round.

Plant in groups or singly, depending on the type of habitat and the size of the herbs being used. For example, in borders, use smaller herbs in groups of three or five and larger ones on their own; in shady areas, plant in drifts; in wet areas, groups of plants of one species are most effective.

Although careful planning is always useful, you do not need to design an elaborate pattern for a herb garden – a small, informal patch close to the kitchen will suffice if you just want to grow a few, well-chosen favourites.

Tiny herb garden
Even in a small container it is possible to have a variety of herbs, such as marjoram, rosemary and lemon verbena.

For those looking for a more attractive layout, one of the simplest is based on the spokes of a wheel, with each segment being used for a different herb. It pays to put a handsome architectural plant in the hub of the wheel to give the garden structure. A clipped boxwood would be good, as would a standard fruit tree, such as a gooseberry, or a standard rose.

The design below will work as well for culinary herbs as for medicinal ones; on the whole, it is best not to mix the two categories.

Much depends on whether your herb garden is ornamental or practical. In either case, if the herb garden is larger than 2m (7ft) in diameter, ensure that the paths between the segments are large enough to walk on, so you can tend the garden easily and conveniently.

If, on the other hand, you have very little space, you can adapt the design to a large-diameter container, simply using fewer herbs in each segment.

Herbs in containers

If you have very little space, there is nothing to prevent you growing some herbs in a window box, for example. Depending on its aspect, the kitchen windowsill can be an excellent spot for cultivating a few culinary herbs, and basil (grown from seed), parsley, chives and thyme will all furnish you with as much as you will need for the kitchen from a relatively small container.

More decorative, larger containers can also be used for more substantial herb displays. Remember that some herbs are quite vigorous, so take care when you combine different herbs in the same container. Mint, for example, spreads by runners and will rapidly take over an entire container, unless you make provision in the shape of a divider. A roof slate or tile, pushed into the container, is a useful divider.

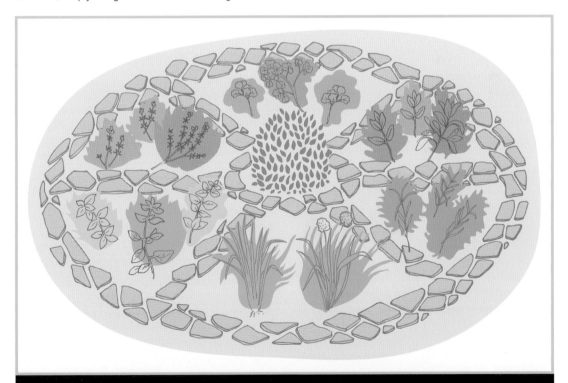

Spoked wheel design
This simple, attractive idea uses six different herbs, one in each segment of the wheel. An ornamental plant is the focal point in the hub.

57

Herbs as companion plants

In the wild you do not often see plants devastated by insect damage or demolished by armies of slugs and snails. Nature has its own balance of complementary plants and predators, which relies on a rich and varied but often crucial mixture of plants and wildlife. Here there is no monoculture – the kind of artificial environment we try to impose on our gardens.

Companion herb plants

Herbs are not only beautiful – they are also useful garden plants. Every plant in the garden affects the plants around it. It may be just by the large leaves offering shade and protection to more delicate plants. Some herbs deter pests and many attract beneficial insects that are valuable pollinators or act as predators of common garden pests.

The most common companion plant combinations are:

Borage, thyme and hyssop	attract bees, which improve crop yield in strawberries and other fruit.
Chamomile	has been found to repel insect attacks, thus improving crop yields.
Chives	have a reputation for preventing black spot on leaves and deterring aphids.
Dill and fennel	attract hoverflies, which then go to work on aphids.
Garlic	with its strong odour is thought to be beneficial to roses.
Mint	the pennyroyals,especially, have been found to be good fly and midge repellents.
Rosemary and thyme	mask the scent of carrots, which deters the carrot fly.
Sage	repels the cabbage white butterfly.
Nasturtium	has an excellent and interesting reputation as a companion plant. It keeps pests away from the vegetable garden, partly owing to the way it attracts aphids away from it. Nasturtium has also been found to repel ants and whitefly. It provides good ground cover, and young leaves and flowers are delicious in salads.
Pot marigold	is a good all-round and attractive companion plant in the vegetable garden. It grows freely, is self-seeding, and deters nematodes in the soil.

Harvesting and storing

Herbs are versatile plants and have many practical applications. Both fresh and dried herbs are valued for their culinary and medicinal properties; dried herbs are a major ingredient of potpourri and make wonderful flower arrangements.

Drying

There are various methods of preserving herbs. For culinary or medicinal use, or for potpourri and dried flower arrangements, drying is often the most suitable method. Herbs that are dried correctly retain their flavour, colour and healing properties. Successful herb drying requires warmth, air flow and shade. Leaves of herbs can be picked for drying at any time. Harvest them when there is plentiful healthy foliage, preferably before the plant flowers, before the heat of the day but after the dew has dried. They are best left on the stalk. After harvesting, remove them from direct sunlight, as

this bleaches them and evaporates the essential oils. Divide and tie the stems into small bunches to hang upside down in a warm, dark and airy place.

Other methods

Herbs that do not dry well, or lose their flavour when dried, are best frozen or preserved in oil. Especially recommended for freezing are basil, tarragon, fennel, chervil, parsley and chives; these can be stored in the freezer in sealed and labelled plastic bags. Chopped leaves and small flowers can also be preserved in ice cubes and look lovely if used in summer drinks.

Drying herbs
Hang herbs in small bunches on a string suspended from the ceiling of a warm, airy room, out of bright light. When the leaves are crisp, rub them off the stalk and seal in a screw-top jar or store in a paper bag.

HERB PROPERTIES

	Culinary	Medicinal	Aromatic	Flowering
Acanthus mollis (Acanthus)		•		•
Achillea millefolium (Yarrow)	•	•		•
Agastache foeniculum (Anise hysop)	•	•	•	•
Ajuga reptans (Bugle)		•		•
Alchemilla vulgaris (Lady's mantle)		•		•
Allium schoenoprasum (Chives)	•			•
Allium sativum (Garlic)	•			
Aloysia triphylla (Lemon verbena)	•	•	•	•
Althaea officinalis (Marsh mallow)	•	•		•
Althaea rosea (Hollyhock)		•		•
Anethum graveolens (Dill)	•			•
Angelica archangelica (Angelica)	•	•		•
Anthemis (Chamomile)		•	•	•
Anthriscus cerefolium (Chervil)	•			
Arctostaphylos uva-ursi (Bearberry)		•		•
Armoracia rusticana (Horseradish)	•	•		
Arnica montana (Arnica)		•		•
Artemisia dracunculus (French tarragon)	•		•	
Atriplex hortensis var. *rubra* (Red orache)	•	•		
Borago officinalis (Borage)	•	•		•
Calamintha grandiflora (Garden calamint)		•	•	•
Calendula officinalis (English marigold, Pot marigold)	•	•		•
Carum carvi (Caraway)	•			•
Chrysanthemum parthenium (Feverfew)		•		•
Cimicifuga racemosa (Black cohosh)		•		•
Coriandrum sativum (Coriander)	•	•		
Dictamnus purpureus (Burning bush)	•		•	•
Digitalis (Foxglove)		•		•
Dipsacus fullonum (Teasel)			•	•
Echinacea purpurea (Purple coneflower)		•		•
Eupatorium purpureum (Joe-Pye weed)		•		
Foeniculum vulgare 'Purpureum' (Bronze fennel)		•		•
Galium odoratum (Sweet woodruff)		•	•	
Galium verum (Lady's bedstraw)		•		•
Gentiana lutea (Yellow gentian)		•		•
Hamamelis virginiana (Witch hazel)		•		•
Helichrysum angustifolium (Curry plant)			•	
Heliotropium arborescens (Heliotrope)			•	•
Hesperis matronalis (Sweet rocket)	•		•	•
Humulus lupulus (Hop)	•	•		
Hypericum perforatum (St John's wort)		•		•

HERB PROPERTIES

	Culinary	Medicinal	Aromatic	Flowering
Hyssopus (Hyssop)	•	•	•	•
Inula helenium (Elecampane)		•		•
Laurus nobilis (Sweet bay)	•			
Lavandula (Lavender)		•	•	•
Levisticum officinale (Lovage)	•	•	•	•
Lobelia syphilitica (Great lobelia)		•		•
Lythrum salicaria (Purple loosestrife)		•		•
Marrubium vulgare (Horehound)		•		•
Melissa officinalis (Lemon balm)	•		•	
Mentha (Mint)	•	•	•	•
Mentha x piperita (Peppermint)	•	•	•	•
Mentha pulegium (Pennyroyal)	•	•		•
Mentha spicata (Spearmint)	•	•	•	
Meum athamanticum (Spignel)	•			•
Monarda (Bergamot)	•		•	•
Myrrhis odorata (Sweet cicely)	•	•		•
Nepeta mussinii (Catmint)	•	•	•	•
Nigella sativa (Fennel flower)	•	•		•
Ocimum (Basil)	•		•	
Oenothera biennis (Evening primrose)	•	•	•	•
Origanum (Oregano)	•	•	•	•
Perilla frutescens (Perilla)	•		•	
Petroselinum crispum (Parsley)	•	•		
Polemonium caeruleum (Jacob's ladder)		•	•	•
Rosa (Rose)			•	•
Rosmarinus officinalis (Rosemary)	•	•		•
Ruta graveolens (Rue)				
Salvia officinalis (Common sage)	•	•		•
Sanguisorba minor (Salad burnet)	•			
Santolina (Santolina)			•	•
Satureja hortensis (Summer savory)	•	•		•
Satureja montana (Winter savory)	•			
Scutellaria lateriflora (Skullcap)		•		•
Symphytum x uplandicum (Russian comfrey)	•			•
Tanacetum balsamita (Costmary)		•		•
Tanacetum vulgare (Tansy)	•	•		•
Thymus vulgaris (Common thyme)	•	•		•
Valeriana officinalis (Valerian)		•	•	•
Verbena (Vervain)		•		•
Viola odorata (Sweet violet)	•	•	•	•
Viola tricolor (Heartsease)	•	•		•

Plant Directory

Ornamental Plants

Flossflower

Ageratum houstonianum

Flowering from early summer onwards, this beautiful half-hardy annual has flower heads which resemble small powder puffs. Shown to their best when edging a formal bedding scheme, they are also good subjects for window boxes and containers.

Use the F1 hybrids now available; these give larger and longer trusses of blooms. The cultivar 'Adriatic' is in this class: its height is 20cm (8in), and the mid-blue flower is produced above light green hairy leaves. Although most cultivars are in the blue range, there are a few whites available.

Care
Flossflower will grow in most ordinary types of soil and tolerates all positions except heavy shade. Avoid planting out too early.

New plants
Sow seeds in trays of seed compost in spring, under glass. When large enough to handle, prick out in the usual way. Plant out in final positions at the end of spring or when the risk of frost has disappeared. Until planting out, try to maintain a temperature of 10–16°C (50–61°F); lower than this will tend to check growth.

H to 30cm (12in)
S to 30cm (12in)

18–20°C
(64–68°F)

Full sun

Love-lies-bleeding
Amaranthus caudatus

This hardy annual has long, tail-like clusters of crimson flowers which can reach 45cm (18in) in length. The flowers are produced on stems up to 105cm (41in) tall. Leaves are ovate in shape and green in colour, the green changing to bronze as the season progresses. *A. caudatus* is used mainly in formal beds as a 'spot' plant to give height. Try them as individual specimens in largish containers or in groups in a mixed border. The long tassel flowers will appear in summer.

Care
Love-lies-bleeding likes a well-cultivated soil in a sunny location. Keep plants well watered in dry periods.

New plants
Raise plants for containers and formal borders by sowing in trays of good seed compost in early spring. Prick off into individual pots under glass and plant out into their final positions in late spring. For borders, sow the seed directly into the open ground in a sunny position in spring. When thinning out seedlings, give plenty of room for development – about 60cm (24in) apart.

H to 120cm (4ft)
S to 45cm (18in)

16–18°C
(61–64°F)

Full sun

China aster

Callistephus chinensis

China asters are useful plants for a bed or border, or in containers, including window boxes. Recent developments have led to a number of useful additions of the dwarf bedding types, and the cultivar 'Milady Dark Rose' is recommended. The rose-coloured double flowers are borne above the dark green foliage. Plants are about 23cm (9in) high, making them ideal bedding plants, especially in areas where wind may cause damage to taller types.

Asters can be affected by various wilt disorders, so avoid planting them in the same spot more than once.

Care

China asters like ordinary well-drained soil and an open and sunny site. Avoid overwatering the plants at any stage.

New plants

Sow seeds under glass in early spring at a temperature of 16°C (61°F). Use any good seed compost for this purpose, and the subsequent pricking out into boxes. Harden them off in the usual way and plant out into flowering positions in early summer, 15cm (6in) apart.

H to 70cm (28in)
S to 30cm (12in)

18–20°C
(64–68°F)

Full sun

Bachelor's buttons, Cornflower

Centaurea cyanus

The common native cornflower, a hardy annual, is a great favourite, but selection and breeding over many years has led to improved strains for the garden. If you decide to grow this plant, try 'Blue Ball', an attractive blue type. Strong 90cm (36in) stems carry the ball-like flowers well above the leaves, which are narrow and lanceolate in shape. Grow in bold groups near godetias and you will have a beautiful contrast of colour during the summer. They are often grown as cut flowers either in the border or in rows in another part of the garden. 'Red Ball' is another attractive variety.

Care

Cornflowers like ordinary well-drained soil and a sunny location. Give support to very tall types.

New plants

Sow seeds in either autumn or spring; those sown in autumn will make larger plants. Take out drills where the plants are to flower, sow the seed and cover. Thin out subsequent seedlings to 45cm (18in). In very cold areas, protect autumn-sown seedlings from frost.

H to 90cm (36in)
S to 60cm (24in)

16–18°C
(61–64°F)

Full sun

Spider plant
Cleome spinosa 'Colour Fountain'

This is a very unusual-looking half-hardy annual; the flowers are spider-shaped and scented. 'Colour Fountain' mixture will include shades of rose, carmine, purple, lilac and pink. Stems reach 60–90cm (24–36in) and carry digitate leaves of five to seven lobes. Some spines may be evident on the undersides of these leaves. This is extremely useful as a 'spot' plant to give height to formal bedding schemes. As a border plant, its height will add character, but care should be taken to position it towards the rear in a sunny place.

Care
Spider plants like light, ordinary soil in full sun. Check for aphids on young plants.

New plants
To flower in summer, seed will need to be sown under glass in spring. Use a seed compost and keep the plant at a temperature of 18°C (64°F). Prick out the seedlings into individual pots, 9cm (3½in) in diameter. Harden off gradually and plant out in late spring.

H to 1.2m (4ft)
S to 45cm (18in)

18–20°C
(64–68°F)

Full sun

Safflower
Carthamus tinctoria

Safflower is also known as false saffron, American saffron and dyer's saffron. Beyond its practical value it is also a decorative annual, with spiny leaves and lovely, thistle-like, golden-yellow flower heads.

Safflower is often grown as an ornamental in the herb garden and is a good border plant. Before sowing in spring, look closely at the seeds, which are shiny, white and shell-like. Sow a small patch of the plant, or several patches if you have room. Its flowers will brighten up the garden from summer into autumn.

The golden flowers of safflower are in great demand as a dye and yield both yellow and a pinkish red; these are used mainly for dyeing silk. The flowers are also blended with talc to make rouge and may be dried for winter decorations. They also provide a saffron substitute for colouring food. However, safflower seeds are most valued today as a source of edible oil. This is rich in linoleic acid, which helps to lower blood cholesterol and is widely sold as a health food product.

Care
Safflowers prefer well-drained soil and require a site in full sunlight.

New plants
Propagate from seed in early spring under cover.

Centaury
Centaurium erythraea

Centaury belongs to the gentian family. This is a tiny, delicate-looking plant with bright rose-pink flowers and few leaves. The flowers are very light-sensitive and open only on bright days. Its medicinal properties are similar to those of *Gentiana lutea* (yellow gentian).

Centaury is not easy to grow in the garden unless the soil is suitable; a poor, alkaline soil is ideal. Centaury grows well in fine grassland on poor soil.

Centaury is a bitter tonic herb used as a tea to stimulate digestion and reduce fevers, and as a bitter flavouring in certain liqueurs.

Care
Centaury prefers dry, rather poor, alkaline soil and a site in full sun.

New plants
The seed is like dust; it is best surface-sown in the autumn where the plants are to grow. This plant self-seeds.

H to 90cm (36in)
S to 23cm (9in)

15–17°C (59–62°F)

Full sun

H to 30cm (12in)
S to10cm (4in)

15–17°C (59–62°F)

Full sun

Larkspur
Consolida ambigua

The larkspur, a favourite cottage-garden flower, was once classified as Delphinium. Larkspur flowers are usually a rich blue or purple, but there are selections of pinks and white.

Although the plant is adaptable, it requires well-drained soil.

The larkspur makes an excellent cut flower, and the dried stems and seed heads are particularly decorative. Although in times past it was used medicinally, larkspur is a poisonous plant. Its chief use is as an insecticide. The juice of the leaves makes a good blue ink or colouring for paper.

Care
Larkspur prefers fertile, well-drained soil and a site in full sun.

New plants
In milder climates, seed it in the autumn for early summer flowering and in spring for colour later in the year. Scatter seed in a border or island bed through other plantings in a random fashion.

Warning All parts of this plant are poisonous.

Tickseed
Coreopsis tinctoria

This native North American plant is often known as tickseed. In some catalogues it is listed under the genus Calliopsis. Tickseed is available only in seed form from herb and wild flower specialists and is very different from the horticultural varieties. It bears jewel-like flower heads of intense golden yellow and rich reds. Each plant is well branched and blooms abundantly over a long period.

The plants grow very bushy, with wiry stems: trim them early in the season to encourage them to bush out and prevent them growing too tall. In the border or island bed, plant them either singly as bright colourful accents or in groups. Wild unselected seed gives a good variety of flower colour. Coreopsis looks stunning with a backdrop of grey and silver foliage.

Coreopsis is an important natural dye plant. The flowers yield yellows, oranges, bronzes and reds.

Care
Coreopsis will thrive in most well-drained, fertile soils and requires a site in full sun.

New plants
Sow coreopsis where it is to grow, or raise it in small plugs or cellular trays and plant out in spring.

H to 90cm (36in)
S to 23cm (9in)

15–17°C (59–62°F)

Full sun

H to 90cm (36in)
S to 30cm (12in)

15–17°C (59–62°F)

Full sun

California poppy
Eschscholzia californica

California poppy is a brilliantly colourful flower. There are many garden forms available in a range of beautiful colours from crimson, through orange-red, to pink-cream and shades of yellow; some have double flowers like 'Ballerina'. The soft grey-green foliage is a perfect foil for the bright blooms.

This plant will survive even the toughest conditions of poor soil and drought. In a mild climate, sow seeds in early autumn to flower early the following year. Sow the seeds in drifts to obtain the full impact of these dazzling poppies. The ideal habitat is gravel or any situation where the soil is poor and light, and receives maximum sun.

In mild climates the California poppy readily self-seeds.

The juice of the plant, which is mildly narcotic, was used by North American Indians as a toothache remedy. Spanish settlers in California used it to make a hair oil.

Care
California poppies prefer poor, sandy, well-drained soil and a site in full sun.

New plants
Sow seeds in spring or autumn; self-seeds.

H to 60cm (24in)
S to 15cm (6in)

18–20°C
(64–68°F)

Full sun

Sunflower
Helianthus annuus 'Sungold'

So many people grow the giant types of this hardy annual that it is often forgotten that a number of the same sunflowers have dwarf counterparts.

'Sungold', only 60cm (24in) tall, can have a worthy place in any border as long as it can benefit from a sunny position. The beautiful double golden-yellow blooms can be up to 15cm (6in) across, and almost ball-shaped. The short stems and longish leaves feel coarse to the touch and the leaves have toothed margins. More showy when grown in groups, they are best suited to the front of a bed.

Care
Check carefully for slug damage at germination time.

New plants
Sow seeds directly into the ground where they are to flower, putting three seeds to a station. When germination is complete, discard the two weakest seedlings, leaving only the strongest. Spacing should be 30cm (12in).

H to 60cm (24in)
S to 15cm (6in)

16–18°C
(61–64°F)

Full sun

Bitter candytuft

Iberis amara

Many gardeners will recall the hardy annual candytuft as among the first plants that they grew in a small plot as children. Still very popular, this strongly aromatic annual looks good along the edge of a well-used pathway where its scent can be appreciated. Use it also in bold drifts towards the front of a border.

Umbrella-shaped flowers form in clusters up to 5cm (2in) across, on stems 15–38cm (6–15in) high, from early summer to autumn. The colours are purple, rose-red and white. Leaves are green, lanceolate and slender-pointed, and may be smothered by the profusion of blooms. As flowering is quick from seed, successive sowings will help to prolong the season of flowering.

Care

This plant prefers ordinary or poor soil and a sunny situation. Keep removing dead flowers.

New plants

Sow thinly in spring where they are to flower. Seedlings should be thinned to 15cm (6in) spacing. It is essential to carry out this process to avoid overcrowding.

H to 30cm (12in)
S to 23cm (9in)

18–20°C
(64–68°F)

Full sun

Mallow

Lavatera trimestris 'Silver Cup'

Mallows have long been grown for their attractive free-flowering effects. The annual cultivar 'Silver Cup' recommended here is one of a number of new hybrids. Glowing pink blooms 8–10cm (3–4in) in diameter are freely produced on stems 60–70cm (24–28in) high and spreading to 75cm (30in). This plant is a member of the hollyhock family, and its leaves are green, ovate and lobed. Flowers grow from the leaf axils and are trumpet-shaped, almost satin in texture, and very pleasing to the eye. Apart from their use in the perennial border, try them towards the back of an annual border.

Care

Mallows like ordinary soil in a sunny and sheltered spot. Give plants plenty of space.

New plants

Sow seeds directly where plants are to flower, in autumn or spring, and cover lightly. Thin out the seedlings of either sowing during late spring to 45cm (18in) intervals. The strong low-branching habit of this plant requires no staking.

Lobelia

Lobelia erinus 'Colour Cascade Mixed'

Probably one of the most widely grown half-hardy annuals, lobelia is very versatile. It includes many shades of blue, rose, red, mauve and white-eyed flowers, which continue to appear until cut down by autumn frosts.

Although best results are obtained from planting in sunny positions, lobelias also succeed in partial shade.

Care

Lobelias prefer ordinary well-cultivated soil. Keep the plants watered in dry weather and feed at intervals.

New plants

These tender annuals need to be sown in heat in late winter or early spring to obtain maximum results. Sow the small seeds very thinly on the surface of a moistened compost seed mixture and do not cover. Germinate in a temperature of 18–21°C (64–70°F). Water carefully to avoid disturbance. Prick out as soon as the seedlings can be handled. Grow on in cooler conditions when established and harden off to plant out when risk of frost has passed.

H to 75cm (30in)
S to 45cm (18in)

15–17°C (59–62°F)

Full sun

H to 15cm (6in)
S to 30cm (12in)

15–17°C (59–62°F)

Full sun or partial shade

Gillyflower, Stock

Matthiola incana 'Giant Imperial Mixed'

Stocks must be one of the most popular scented annuals. En masse this fragrance can be overpowering, however, so do not overplant. The 'Giant Imperial Mixed' always provides reliable flowers with a high percentage of doubles. Stems 38–50cm (15–20in) tall carry a profusion of pink, white, lilac, purple and crimson spikes of flowers from early summer onwards. Grey-green soft narrow leaves are formed under the flower heads and give a pleasing and attractive contrast.

Care

Stock will tolerate most soils, but they should preferably be alkaline. It requires a sunny position, but tolerates partial shade. Kill caterpillars at once.

New plants

Sow seeds for summer flowering during the early spring under glass at a temperature of 13°C (55°F). Use a loam-based compost for sowing and pricking out seedlings. Grow on at a lower temperature and harden off before planting out 23cm (9in) apart.

H to 50cm (20in)
S to 30cm (12in)

18–20°C
(64–68°F)

Full sun

Baby blue eyes

Nemophila menziesii, Nemophila insignis

This is one of the more notable hardy annuals from California. Plants grow to a height of 23cm (9in) and have spreading slender stems on which deeply cut, feathery, light green leaves are carried. Appearing from early summer, the flowers are buttercup-shaped and of a beautiful sky blue with a very striking white centre. Each bloom measures 4cm (1½in) in diameter. This species will tolerate partial shade; use it where a low planting is required.

Before sowing, fork in organic matter if your soil is on the light side. This will ensure that moisture is retained in hot dry spells so that plants can survive.

Care
Baby blue eyes likes ordinary but moist soil. It requires a site in full sun or partial shade. Water freely during dry weather.

New plants
Sow seeds directly where they are to flower, in early spring. Take out shallow drills and only lightly cover the seed. Thin out seedlings to 15cm (6in) apart. In mild regions autumn sowings will provide plants for flowering in late spring.

H to 23cm (9in)
S to 45cm (15in)

16–18°C
(61–64°F)

Full sun or partial shade

Tobacco plant

Nicotiana × sanderae 'Nicki Hybrids' F1

The Nicki F1 Hybrids are a lovely mixture of colours, including red, pink, rose, lime green and white. Individual blooms are up to 6cm (2½in) long, formed into loose clusters. Stems bearing the flowers carry large oblong leaves of a light green. This strain is dwarf and reaches only about 25cm (10in) in height. The blooms of this free-flowering half-hardy annual are sweetly fragrant. Use as a bedding plant for formal beds or borders, beneath a window, or on a patio or in a yard where the scent can be appreciated, especially in the evening hours.

Care

Tobacco plant prefers rich, well-drained soil and a site in full sun or partial shade. Do not plant out too early.

New plants

Sow seeds under glass in early spring, in a temperature of 18°C (64°F). Seeds should be scattered thinly on top of prepared pots or trays of a seed compost. Prick out in the usual way. Harden off and plant out in early summer, 23cm (9in) apart.

H to 38cm (15in)
S to 30cm (12in)

15–17°C
(59–62°F)

Full sun or partial shade

Poppy
Papaver

Of all the many members of the poppy family, the genus Papaver is the largest. The red corn poppy, or Flanders poppy (*Papaver rhoeas*), is immortalised as the Poppy of Remembrance, and is the most common and best loved.

The seeds of the corn poppy can remain viable in the soil for many decades, but the earth must be disturbed or cultivated for the plant to appear. It will not grow well among established thick vegetation. Seed a patch of waste ground for a quick and colourful display, perhaps with other bright cornfield flowers, such as *Anthemis arvensis* (chamomile) and *Centaurea cyanus* (cornflower).

P. somniferum (opium poppy) is a larger plant. The flowers are big and handsome, in a range of colours with a large dark blotch at the base. Many varieties have been developed with double, peony-like or fringed, carnation-like flowers in various shades. The decorative opium poppy self-seeds readily. In some areas it is illegal to grow this plant. This is an invaluable medicinal plant, today utilised in the manufacture of painkillers such as codeine and morphine.

Care
Poppies will grow in most soils, including chalk. They like a site in full sun.

New plants
Sow seeds in late summer, autumn or early spring; self-seeds.

H to 90cm (36in)
S to 23cm (9in)

16–18°C
(61–64°F)

Full sun

Petunia

Petunia × hybrida

In a good sunny summer the petunia is second to none for its profusion of colour and versatility of use. Flowers are trumpet-shaped, up to 10cm (4in) across. Leaves and stems will be a mid- to dark green. Leaves vary in size but are usually ovate. The whole plant feels sticky to the touch. Use these petunias for a range of purposes, including formal bedding, borders, containers, window boxes and hanging baskets.

Petunias are really half-hardy perennials, but are invariably grown as half-hardy annuals. All petunias love a sunny position and benefit from being grown in a well-cultivated soil. Avoid having the soil over-rich, as this can lead to a lot of growth and few flowers.

Care
Petunias prefer ordinary well-cultivated soil and a sunny location. Remove faded flowers regularly.

New plants
Seeds will need to be sown under glass in early spring. Sow thinly on top of a seed compost in pots or trays. Prick out the seedlings into trays, harden off and plant out in early summer. Spacing will depend on the cultivar you choose.

H to 30cm (12in)
S to 1.2m (4ft)

16–18°C
(61–64°F)

Full sun

Phacelia

Phacelia tanacetifolia

Phacelia has recently come to the notice of gardeners as a good green manure crop. It is also a superb beekeeper's plant, being especially attractive to the honeybee.

This plant has the advantage of rapid growth, providing quick ground cover and a shallow, extensive root system that produces a fine soil. Dig in, or prolong its life span by cutting before flowering. Beekeepers should leave the plant to flower over a long period, and it will then self-seed.

Phacelia is extremely decorative. Sow a good-sized patch in any area of the garden that you do not intend to use for a few months and wait for a wonderful display of colour.

Care
Phacelia will tolerate most soils, but prefers some moisture. It needs a site in full sun or partial shade.

New plants
Sow seeds in spring after frosts have finished; self-seeds. In mild areas phacelia will overwinter as young self-sown seedlings; in colder areas, however, it should be sown anew each year by broadcasting the seeds and raking in. The more thickly it is sown, the lower it will grow.

H to 90cm (36in)
S to 30cm (12in)

18–20°C
(64–68°F)

Full sun or
partial shade

Annual phlox

Phlox drummondii 'Carnival'

An easy-to-grow, half-hardy annual, *Phlox drummondii* will give a succession of colour throughout the summer. For a really bright display, try the cultivar 'Carnival'; this mixture has pink, rose, salmon, scarlet, blue and violet flowers. The flowers are borne on stems 30cm (12in) high, which carry light green lanceolate leaves. Blooms are produced in early summer as dense heads up to 10cm (4in) in diameter; each individual flower is rounded. These plants are ideally suited for low-growing areas of the garden, especially the rock garden.

Care
Phlox like ordinary well-drained soil and an open, sunny site. Dead-head to prolong flowering.

New plants
In spring, sow seeds under glass in a temperature of 16°C (61°F). Use any good growing medium for sowing. Sow the seeds thinly and cover them lightly. Prick out the young seedlings, when large enough to handle, into trays. Harden off and plant out in flowering positions in early summer at 23cm (9in) intervals.

H to 30cm (12in)
S to 15cm (6in)

16–18°C
(61–64°F)

Full sun

Nasturtium
Tropaeolum majus

The nasturtium, or Indian cress, is among the brightest and most colourful of garden flowers. This decorative herb makes an excellent companion plant for the vegetable garden. The dwarf form looks attractive around shrubs, in the border, or in a container.

The vivid flowers make a colourful decoration for green salads, and the leaves add a peppery flavour. The seeds can be pickled when still green. The nasturtium also has some medicinal properties. The seeds are antibacterial and an infusion of the leaves is used to treat infections of the genito-urinary tract and bronchitis.

Care
This plant prefers dry to moisture-retaining loam and requires a site in full sun or partial shade.

New plants
Propagate by sowing seeds in spring.

H to 30cm (12in)
S to 45cm (18in)

18–20°C
(64–68°F)

Full sun or
partial shade

Verbena

Verbena × hybrida 'Florist Mixed'

This half-hardy perennial is invariably grown as a half-hardy annual. The variety 'Florist Mixed' provides a diverse colour range. The stems, 23cm (9in) in height, tend to spread and make a mat. The rainbow shades of the flowers are produced above the foliage, which is dark green – this gives a jewel-like effect. This perennial is very useful as a front plant for window boxes, containers or flowerbeds and borders.

Plant in a good-sized clump to obtain the best and longest effect of flowering. Those for containers and window boxes can be planted out slightly earlier as long as they are in sheltered positions. Spacing should be 23cm (9in) apart.

Care
Verbenas will grow happily in any fertile soil in a sunny position. Water plants freely in very dry weather.

New plants
Sow seeds in pots or trays in early spring under glass. Keep at a temperature of 16°C (61°F). Use any good growing medium. Prick out the young seedlings, as soon as they are ready, into trays. Harden off and plant out into flowering positions in early summer.

Zinnia

Zinnia elegans 'Hobgoblin Mixed'

The 'Hobgoblin' mixture of this half-hardy annual has a range of colour in shades of red, pink, yellow and gold.

Zinnias make good, bushy, compact plants. The stems are about 25cm (10in) long and branched. The leaves are ovate, pointed and light green. Both stems and leaves are covered with stiff hairs. These plants are ideal for borders and beds in a bright, sunny situation.

Care
Zinnias will tolerate any ordinary well-drained soil. They require an open, sunny position. Avoid overwatering at any stage.

New plants
As a tender half-hardy annual, this plant will need to be raised from seed under glass in spring. Sow seeds in any good compost that is free-draining. Keep at a temperature of 16°C (61°F). Prick out seedlings into individual peat pots; this will avoid handling the stems at a later date, which can be damaging. Grow on in the usual way and harden off at the end of spring. Plant out carefully in early summer, 23cm (9in) apart.

H to 23cm (9in)
S to 23cm (9in)

18–20°C (64–68°F)

Full sun

H to 25cm (10in)
S to 15cm (6in)

15–17°C (59–62°F)

Full sun

Japanese anemone,
Japanese windflower, windflower
Anemone × hybrida

Of all the many anemones, the best-known are the many hybrids of the hardy, herbaceous perennial *Anemone* x *hybrida* (also known as *A. japonica*). These vary in height from 45cm (18in) to 1.2m (4ft), and their individual flowers vary in size from 4cm (1½in) to 6cm (2½in) across, each with five or more petals. Each flower has a central boss of yellow stamens. The stems are clothed with vine-like leaves. Their roots are like stiff black leather bootlaces. Choose from the following selection: 'Bressingham Glow', a semi-double rosy red, 45cm (18in) tall; 'Luise Uhink', white, 90cm (36in); 'September Charm', single soft pink, 45cm (18in); 'White Queen', 90cm–1.2m (36in–4ft); and 'Honorine Jobert', white, 1.2m (4ft).

Care
Anemones like good ordinary soil. Good drainage is needed and, preferably, a sunny position.

New plants
Propagate by cutting the roots into 4–5cm (1½–2in) lengths and inserting them in a deep box filled with compost and sand mixture.

H to 1.2m (4ft)
S to 30cm (12in)

18–20°C
(64–68°F)

Full sun

Italian aster, Italian starwort

Aster amellus

This colourful herbaceous perennial has large solitary flowers with golden-yellow centres and several clusters to each strong branching stem. The grey-green foliage and the stems are rough when handled. These plants form a woody rootstock.

Four varieties to choose from are: 'King George', soft blue-violet 8cm (3in) flowers with golden-yellow centres, introduced 70 years ago; the 60cm (24in) tall 'Nocturne', with lavender-lilac flowers; the large-flowered pink 'Sonia', 60cm (24in); and the compact dwarf aster, 45cm (18in) tall, 'Violet Queen'.

They object to winter wetness and are happiest in a good, well-drained, retentive soil. They are best planted in spring.

Care

They need retentive well-drained soil in a sunny position. Do not let them have wet roots in winter.

New plants

Propagate by basal cuttings in spring or by division where possible.

H to 60cm (24in)
S to 45cm (18in)

16–18°C
(62–64°F)

Full sun

Michaelmas daisy

Aster novi-belgii

Michaelmas daisies are superb herbaceous perennials with large and colourful daisy-like flower heads in September and October. They need to be grown in fertile soil, as they soon exhaust the ground. Position in full sun.

There are many varieties to choose from; some of these are: 'Carnival', with semi-double, cherry-red flowers 60cm (24in) high; 'Freda Ballard', with semi-double, rich red flowers 90cm (36in) high; and 'Royal Ruby', with semi-double, rich ruby, early flowers 50cm (20in) high.

Dwarf varieties include: 'Jenny', with double red flowers 30cm (12in) high; 'Professor Kippenburg', with clear blue flowers 30cm (12in) high; and 'Snowsprite', with white, late flowers 30cm (12in) high.

Care
These plants need a fertile soil in a sunny position. If mildew attacks, spray flowers with sulphur.

New plants
Propagate these plants by dividing the roots in spring, every three years. Replant only the healthiest pieces.

False goat's beard

Astilbe × arendsii

Astilbes are one of the most decorative hardy herbaceous perennials. The *arendsii* hybrids vary from white, through pale pink, deep pink, coral and red, to magenta. Not only are they good garden plants, but they also force well under glass in an unheated greenhouse. The foliage varies from light to dark green, with some of purplish and reddish purple shades. The fluffy panicles of flowers are held on erect stems 60–90cm (24–36in) tall, but dwarf varieties are only 45cm (18in).

They will grow in full sun or partial shade and thrive in most soils. They have a long flowering period and their rigid erect stems do not require staking. There are too many varieties to mention, but all are worth a place in any garden.

Care
These plants require a moist, fertile soil and a site in full sunshine, although they will tolerate partial shade. Do not cut old flower stems back before spring.

New plants
Propagate by division in spring. Alternatively, roots may be divided in autumn and potted for forcing or spring planting.

H to 90cm (36in)
S to 90cm (36in)

18–20°C (64–68°F)

Full sun

H to 90cm (36in)
S to 60cm (24in)

16–18°C (61–64°F)

Full sun or partial shade

Plumbago

Ceratostigma

This group consists of about eight tender, deciduous perennials and shrubs from eastern Africa and eastern Asia. These plants, commonly known as plumbagos, are grown for their attractive autumn foliage and pretty blue flowers. They are excellent for growing in the rock garden or flower border. *Ceratostigma griffithii* is a low-growing, semi-evergreen plant with deep blue flowers and bright red autumn foliage that persists well into the winter. After a harsh winter, this plant may not blossom. *C. willmottianum* (Chinese plumbago) is a deciduous shrub that grows about 1m (3ft) high. The blue flowers are produced from mid-summer until autumn, when the leaves become stained with red.

Care

Plumbagos can be grown in mild climates only. They should be planted in the spring, in dry, well-drained soil in a sunny location. In the spring the old flowering growths should be pruned back.

New plants

These plants may be lifted, separated and replanted in the spring. Cuttings may also be taken in the summer and either inserted in very sandy soil outside and covered with a bell jar, or placed in a greenhouse or frame.

H to 1m (3ft)
S to 1m (3ft)

20–25°C
(68–77°F)

Full sun

Turtlehead

Chelone obliqua

This rather strange-looking herbaceous perennial derives its popular name from the unusual shape of its flowers. It is a close relation of the penstemons and is sometimes confused with them. Its dark green leaves are broad to oblong in shape, 5–20cm (2–8in) long, and arranged in pairs, the last two being just below the erect crowded truss of rosy purple flowers. The square stems are 60–90cm (24–36in) tall. Provided it is given a sunny position in the border, this plant will produce blooms for several weeks in autumn. The flowers are very weather-resistant, which is useful in wet seasons. Its roots have a spreading habit.

Care

Chelones prefer fertile, well-drained soil and a position in partial shade. They may crowd out less tough growing plants.

New plants

Propagate by seed sown in spring under glass in a temperature of 13–18°C (55–64°F), or in late spring without heat in a cold frame. Also, propagate by division of roots in spring or in late autumn as soon as flowers fade.

Shasta daisy

Chrysanthemum maximum

The Shasta daisy, a native of the Pyrenees, is a must for any herbaceous perennial border. The height varies from 60cm (24in) to 90cm (36in). Flowers are single or double, with plain or fringed petals. Because of the large flat heads, rain and wind can soon knock plants over. Short peasticks should be inserted in the ground before the plants are too advanced.

One of the best-known varieties is 'Esther Read', 45cm (18in) tall, with pure white, fully double flowers. 'Wirral Pride' is a 90cm (36in) beauty with large anemone-centred blooms, and another variety is the fully double, white-flowered 'Wirral Supreme', 80cm (32in) high. If you prefer a large, fully double, frilly flowered variety, plant 'Droitwich Beauty', 80–90cm (32–36in) tall. The creamy yellow 'Mary Stoker' is 80cm (32in) tall.

Care

Shasta daisies like any good fertile soil in a sunny position. Be sure to provide support.

New plants

Propagate by softwood cuttings in summer, or by division in autumn or spring.

H to 90cm (36in)
S to 60cm (24in)

15–17°C (59–62°F)

Partial shade

H to 90cm (36in)
S to 60cm (24in)

15–17°C (59–62°F)

Full sun

Lily of the valley

Convallaria majalis

Lily of the valley is still an old-fashioned favourite, popular for its delightful hanging, and very fragrant, bell-shaped blooms.

This plant is always at its best grown in drifts, in a woodland setting, but if there are no trees or shrubs to cast shade, a north-facing wall is suitable. The clear white of the flowers and the fresh green foliage look best against a dark background. In ideal conditions the rhizomes will spread rapidly and form a large patch. Plant the crowns well below the surface.

Lily of the valley has for centuries been used medicinally. The flowers are used as a perfume base.

Care

Lily of the valley prefers humus-rich, well-drained, moisture-retaining to dry soil. It requires a site in shade or partial shade.

New plants

Divide in the autumn or after flowering.

Warning All parts of this plant are poisonous.

H to 30cm (12in)
S to 15cm (6in)

16–18°C
(61–64°F)

Shade or
partial shade

Montbretia

Crocosmia masonorum

This South African cormous plant has sword-like leaves with pronounced centre spines, and grows to 75cm (30in) tall. The flowers are bright orange, 2.5cm (1in) long, and the plant will give a succession of blooms from mid-summer.

These plants can be invasive; confine them by planting in a bottomless container sunk into the ground. The plants need a well-drained soil, but keep it moist during summer droughts. The flowers are often used for cutting; if they are left on the plants, remove them as soon as they die. Cut off dead leaves before the new ones appear in spring. They are normally pest- and disease-free.

Care
Montbretia likes well-drained sandy soil and a sunny location.

New plants
The corms should be planted in spring, 8cm (3in) deep and 15cm (6in) apart, in a sunny position. Corms should be lifted every few years; divide after flowering and before new growth appears.

H to 75cm (30in)
S to 1m (3ft)

18–20°C
(64–68°F)

Full sun

Delphinium
Delphinium elatum

These are hardy herbaceous perennials, well known for decorating borders with spires of flowers during June and July. The true species is seldom grown, and the forms now cultivated are *Delphinium elatum* (large-flowered type) and *D. belladonna* types.

   The *elatum* plants develop long, upright spires of flowers on plants up to 2.5m (8ft) high, although dwarf forms, such as 'Baby Doll' and 'Blue Fountains', and medium-height forms, such as 'Blue Nile' and 'Cressida', are available.

   Derived from the *elatum* are the *belladonna* varieties. They are smaller at between 1m (3ft) and 1.5m (5ft) high. They have a lax, graceful habit and beautifully cupped florets.

Care
These summer- and autumn-flowering plants prefer deep, rich, well-drained and moisture-retentive soil. They require a site in full sun. Avoid cold, wet soils and plant in spring.

New plants
Propagate delphiniums by division or by cuttings rooted in a cold frame in spring.

H to 2.5m (8ft)
S to 50cm (20in)

18–20°C
(64–68°F)

Full sun

Pink
Dianthus 'Dynasty'

'Dynasty' is a range of double-flowered dianthus with flowers that have the appearance of mini-carnations. The plants bear well-branched, strong-stemmed, upright flowers that are lightly scented, and come in four colours – a rich purple, a velvety red, 'Rose Lace', which is a lovely deep rose with a fine white outer edge, and 'White Blush', which has white flowers with a rose-pink blush that fades as the flower matures.

Pinks have long been favourites with cottage gardeners, but their charm and scent mean that they are a good addition to any garden.

Care
Frost-tolerant and requiring minimal maintenance, 'Dynasty' dianthus like full sun and well-drained, neutral soil.

New plants
Propagate perennial dianthus from cuttings in summer.

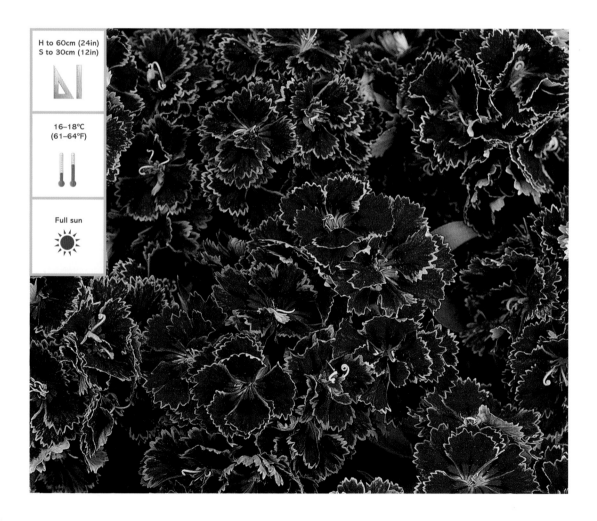

H to 60cm (24in)
S to 30cm (12in)

16–18°C
(61–64°F)

Full sun

Globe thistle

Echinops humilis 'Taplow Blue'

Globe thistles are herbaceous perennials with round drumstick heads in varying tones of blue. They are coarse-growing with stout, rough, wiry stems and deeply cut, greyish, spiny foliage, woolly beneath. Bees are especially attracted to the globular flowers. The flower heads can be dried for winter decoration. The variety 'Taplow Blue' is 1.5m (5ft) tall, with dark blue globular flowers that have a metallic steely lustre. A variety with a slightly richer blue is 'Veitch's Blue'.

These hardy herbaceous perennials can be grown successfully in the poorest of soils, whether sand or chalk, but should be well drained.

Care
Globe thistles will grow happily in any soil, so long as it is situated in full sun. Provide a good depth of soil, as the thong-like roots of this plant are very penetrating.

New plants
Propagate by root cuttings in late autumn or winter, or by division in autumn or spring.

H to 1.5m (5ft)
S to 60cm (24in)

18–20°C
(64–68°F)

Full sun

Fuchsia
Fuchsia

One of the most widely cultivated plants in the world, fuchsias are beautiful and exotic. There are thousands of different types of this plant, which was originally bred from a handful of wild species found in Mexico, the West Indies and New Zealand.

Colours vary from pinks, purples, whites and reds to sober or flashy multi-coloured mixtures. Several (for example, *Fuchsia magellanica*) can even be grown as hedges.

Fuchsias basically divide into the hardy types that can be left outside all year; the bushy or upright and tender kind for pots; and the dangling, trailing ones for hanging baskets.

All fuchsia flowers have three parts: the upper tube; the sepals beneath that often point out like wings; and the corolla (the petals) – the skirt-like growth underneath the sepals. Each can be a different colour in some varieties.

Care
Most fuchsias require little care, apart from a spring pruning to generate new growth. Situate in full sun.

New plants
Grow new young plants in rich, moist compost and pinch out the young shoots regularly to encourage bushiness. These can be used as cuttings.

Spotted cranesbill
Geranium maculatum

Spotted cranesbill is a pretty woodland flower of North America with clear lilac-blue flowers that appear in late spring, earlier than those of most other hardy geraniums. The Latin name, *maculatum*, means 'spotted' and refers to the pale spots that develop on the leaves. The decorative foliage turns to beautiful autumn colours of fawn, orange and red.

Although it is a woodland plant, cranesbill will grow in the garden and forms a dense ground cover. It has thick rhizomes, which in time form good-sized clumps. This plant requires some moisture to do well, but it will also withstand a certain amount of drought. It readily self-seeds, and the seed pods, constructed like catapults, eject their contents when ripe.

The powdered rhizome is used medicinally for a range of ailments, including diarrhoea and sore throats, and to stop bleeding.

Care
Spotted cranesbill prefers humus-rich, moisture-retaining loam and a site in full sun or partial shade.

New plants
Sow seeds or divide plants in the autumn.

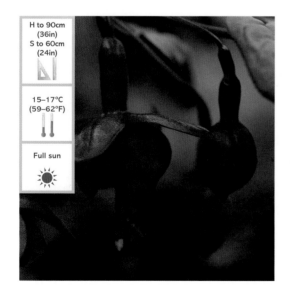

H to 90cm (36in)
S to 60cm (24in)

15–17°C (59–62°F)

Full sun

H to 60cm (24in)
S to 60cm (24in)

15–17°C (59–62°F)

Full sun or partial shade

Baby's breath
Gypsophila paniculata

The flower heads of this perennial are a mass of small feathery flowers, white or pink. The glaucous leaves are also small. The branching flower heads are used by flower arrangers to add a light cloud effect to floral arrangements. *Gypsophila paniculata* 'Bristol Fairy' is the best double form, at 90cm (36in) tall.

As gypsophilas are deep-rooted, the ground must be well prepared before planting; it should be double dug. To do this, dig a trench by removing the first spit (spade's depth) of soil and break up the spit below with a fork. Remove the first spit of soil from a second trench and transfer it to the first trench. Then break up the bottom of the second trench and fill it with the first spit from the first trench. Enrich the ground with well-rotted farmyard manure or well-rotted garden compost. Provided they have full sun and well-drained soil, gypsophilas should be no trouble.

Care
Baby's breath prefers well-drained, preferably limy, soil and a sunny location. Insert a few peasticks for support.

New plants
Propagate 'Bristol Fairy' by taking softwood cuttings in late spring to very early summer.

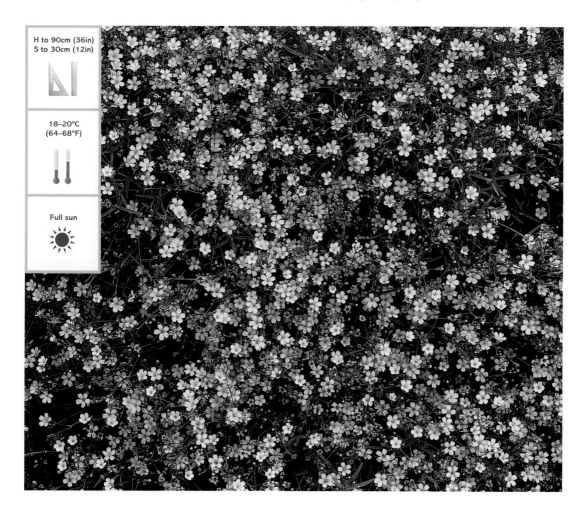

H to 90cm (36in)
S to 30cm (12in)

18–20°C
(64–68°F)

Full sun

Day lily
Hemerocallis fulva

The day lily is so called because each flower opens for only a day, but the plant has blooms in succession over a long period. It enjoys a certain amount of moisture and, if the soil is damp enough through the summer, will grow naturally with grass, to make an exotic flowering meadow.

Hemerocallis fulva is a vigorous plant that needs space to spread. Grown alone among shrubs in light shade or full sun, or beside a stream, it can make a spectacular sight. Other day lilies are less vigorous.

The Chinese considered the flower buds of this plant a delicacy. Other parts of the day lily, however, are thought to be potentially toxic. The root was used in traditional Chinese medicine for various ailments, and is believed to be antibacterial.

Care
Day lilies like fertile, moist or moisture-retaining soil and must be situated in full sun or partial shade.

New plants
Divide in spring or autumn.

H to 1.2m (4ft)
S to 50cm (20in)

16–18°C
(61–64°F)

Full sun or
partial shade

Red-hot poker
Kniphofia

Kniphofias are herbaceous perennials that will come through most winters. To ensure their safety, tie the foliage into a kind of wigwam in winter, to keep the crowns dry. The flowers are carried on stout stems. One beauty is 'Little Maid', about 60cm (24in) tall, with attractive creamy flower spikes. *Kniphofia galpinii* 'Bressingham Seedlings' produces orange spikes, 45–90cm (18–36in) tall.

Kniphofias require a fairly rich soil with ample humus, such as rotted manure or garden compost. After clumps have been divided, do not allow them to dry out before or after planting. A mulch of rotted manure or garden compost should be given annually in spring, otherwise they can remain untouched for several years. Plant them three or four to the square metre (square yard).

Care
These early summer- to autumn-flowering plants prefer rich, retentive, well-drained soil in a site in full sun. Protect crowns during winter.

New plants
Propagate by division in spring.

H to 90cm (36in)
S to 40cm (16in)

18–20°C
(64–68°F)

Full sun

Lupin
Lupinus polyphyllus

Lupins enjoy sun and well-drained soil. Take care to avoid lime and heavy, wet, clay soils. Before planting, see that the ground is well cultivated, with an ample supply of well-rotted farmyard manure or garden compost. On well-drained soils, plant in autumn; otherwise, wait until spring.

With established plants, restrict the number of flower spikes to between five and seven, when stems are about 30cm (12in) high. Give a light spraying of plain water in the evening during dry springs. As a rule, staking is not necessary. Named varieties can be obtained, but the Russell hybrids have a good mixture of colours and vary in height from 90cm (36in) to 1.2m (4ft). In very windy gardens, sow the dwarf 'Lulu' lupin. This is only 60cm (24in) tall.

Care
These early summer-flowering plants prefer light sandy loam in full sun. Remove faded flower heads to prevent them forming seeds which will take strength from the plant.

New plants
Propagate by basal cuttings in early spring, when 8–10cm (3–4in) long; insert in a cold frame.

H to 1.2m (4ft)
S to 75cm (30in)

18–20°C
(64–68°F)

Full sun

Creeping Jenny
Lysimachia nummularia

Creeping Jenny has many other old country names, the most common of which is moneywort, referring to the round, penny-like leaves, and possibly to the golden flowers that resemble cascading coins.

This is a decorative ground-cover plant for moist or wet ground that gets some shade. It thrives if grown in a woodland-edge or pond-edge site, and provides early green ground cover followed by profuse, brilliant gold flowers. A cover of leaf-mould mulch, about 15cm (6in) deep, every autumn will do it good. Allow this plant space to spread. In warmer climates creeping Jenny can become too rampant for the small garden.

An old medicinal herb, it was supposed to have many virtues and was used as a compress for wounds.

Care
Creeping Jenny prefers moist, humus-rich loam. It requires a site in shade or partial shade.

New plants
Divide in spring.

Peony
Paeonia officinalis

The peony is a robust shrub that was developed for its beautiful blooms. Most of the forms of peony now available bear spectacular double flowers in many colourful shades.

Essentially a plant of the woodland edge, the peony looks its best associated with trees and shrubs. Grow it as a specimen plant, and give it space and a rich, woodland soil, with plenty of leaf mould. The peony will withstand periods of drought in summer, drawing on reserves in its thick rootstock.

Paeonia officinalis, sometimes called the apothecaries' peony, is an early cultivated plant, named by the ancient Greeks after Paen, the physician to the gods. The plant is still valued medicinally by the Chinese.

Care
Peonies prefer humus-rich, moisture-retaining but well-drained soil and a site in partial shade or full sun (avoid early-morning sun).

New plants
Sow seeds in autumn; divide roots with a bud in early autumn.

Warning The flowers are poisonous.

H to 4cm (1in)
S indefinite

15–17°C
(59–62°F)

Shade or partial shade

H to 90cm
(36in)
S to 50cm
(20in)

15–17°C
(59–62°F)

Full sun or partial shade

Passionflower

Passiflora incarnata

Passionflower must be among the most exotic of all flowers. It makes a superb dense cover for sheds or fences, and can also be trained to grow up through a large tree. When mature, the plant produces many flowers, followed by edible fruits.

In a small garden or on a patio, growth will be restricted. The plant can be grown successfully in a container. *Passiflora incarnata* will not stand temperatures below freezing; the species *P. caerulea* is a hardier plant and more suitable for northern climates.

Far from arousing 'passion', as its name suggests, *P. incarnata* is in fact a sedative and tranquilliser with a mild narcotic effect. It is still much used in European herbal medicine.

Care
Passionflowers prefer fertile and well-drained soil, and a site in partial shade.

New plants
Pre-soak seeds, sow in spring; keep moist.

H to 9.1m (30ft)
S indefinite

18–20°C
(64–68°F)

Partial shade

Jerusalem sage
Phlomis russeliana

This handsome weed-smothering plant, or ground cover, has large, rough, puckered, heart-shaped, felty, sage-like grey-green leaves. Among the foliage, stout flower spikes, 75–90cm (30–36in) high, carry whorls of soft, rich yellow hooded flowers in early summer to mid-summer. The attractive seed heads can be used successfully in flower arrangements, whether green or dried.

Care
These summer-flowering plants like an ordinary, well-drained soil and a sunny location. Plant phlomis against a suitable background, such as a red-leaved Japanese maple.

New plants
Propagation of this plant is by seed, cutting or division, in spring or autumn.

H to 90cm (36in)
S to 75cm (30in)

18–20°C
(64–68°F)

Full sun

Jacob's ladder

Polemonium caeruleum

Jacob's ladder is so called because of the ladder-like formation of its bright green leaves. This is a cottage flower that has been grown for many centuries in country gardens.

Jacob's ladder requires moisture in the soil to flourish and grows well in partially shaded areas. It associates well with water, and with trees and shrubs. For a long flowering, cut down the stems before they go to seed so that more will grow. One stem will be more than adequate for self-seeding, since seeds are produced in abundance.

In times past the herb was used to treat fevers, headaches, epilepsy and nervous complaints.

Care
Jacob's ladder prefers humus-rich, moist to moisture-retaining, calcareous loam. It requires a site in full sun, although it will tolerate partial shade.

New plants
Sow seeds in spring or autumn; divide roots in spring; self-seeds.

H to 90cm (36in)
S to 50cm (20in)

18–20°C
(64–68°F)

Full sun

Obedient plant
Physostegia virginiana

This hardy herbaceous perennial is called the obedient plant because its flowers have hinged stalks and can be moved from side to side, remaining as altered on their square stems. The long, narrow, dark green, glossy leaves are toothed and grow in four columns. The dull rose-pink flowers terminate the square tapering spikes, 45–105cm (18–41in) tall. They bloom from summer to autumn, until the frosts spoil their beauty. Physostegia has vigorous stoloniferous rootstocks that spread underground.

There are several good varieties: 'Rose Bouquet' has pinkish mauve trumpet flowers and is 60cm (35in) to 1.2m (4ft) tall; 'Summer Snow' is pure white and about

75cm (30in) high; and 'Vivid' bears rose-crimson flowers on stalks 30–45cm (12–18in) tall.

Care
This late summer-flowering plant likes any good fertile soil and a site in sun or partial shade. Give this plant sufficient moisture during dry summer weather.

New plants
Sow seeds in spring or autumn; divide roots in spring. This plant self-seeds. Propagate by division in spring or by root cuttings in winter.

H to 105cm (41in)
S to 70cm (28in)

15–17°C
(59–62°F)

Full sun or
partial shade

Primrose

Primula vulgaris

The primrose is one of the earliest spring flowers. It once grew in great profusion in the wild, but many of its natural habitats have now been destroyed. Primroses enjoy a rich soil with moisture and a thick mulch of leaf mould. They always look their best associated with woodland and can be successfully naturalised in wooded areas and partial shade, or in grass, which should be left uncut until after seeding in mid-summer. Primrose stems curve over to the ground when the seeds are ripe. If seed is sown when fresh, germination will occur during the autumn; otherwise, it needs the winter cold to stimulate germination.

The plant has medicinal properties similar to those of the cowslip. The flowers can be candied.

Care
Primroses prefer humus-rich, moisture-retaining loam and a site in shade or partial shade.

New plants
Sow seeds as soon as they ripen or stratify. Divide in the autumn.

Coneflower

Rudbeckia fulgida

This is one of the most useful border and cut flowers in late summer and autumn. Erect 60cm (24in) stems rise from leafy clumps, displaying several large, golden-yellow, daisy-like flowers with short blackish purple central discs or cones, hence the name coneflower. The narrow leaves are rather rough to handle. Other garden forms of *Rudbeckia fulgida* are the free-flowering *R. f. deamii*, 90cm (36in) tall, and 'Goldsturm', which, above its bushy growth, has stems 60cm (24in) tall carrying chrome-yellow flowers with dark brown cones. Rudbeckias make good cut flowers and blend very well with *Aster amellus* 'King George'.

Care
This late summer- and autumn-flowering plant prefers moist, fertile soil in a site in full sun. Do not let plants dry out during the summer.

New plants
Propagate by dividing the plants in autumn or spring.

H to 20cm (8in)
S to 20cm (8in)

18–20°C (64–68°F)

Shade or partial shade

H to 90cm (36in)
S to 90cm (36in)

16–18°C (61–64°F)

Full sun

Ice plant
Sedum spectabile 'Autumn Joy'

The name ice plant probably originated because this species has glaucous glistening foliage. The leaves are opposite or in threes and clasp stout erect stems 30–60cm (12–24in) high. Above these stems are borne flat, plate-like, unbranched flowers. *Sedum spectabile* has pale pink blooms. The varieties 'Carmen' and 'Meteor' are a deeper pink, and 'Brilliant' is a deep rose-pink. 'Autumn Joy' is at first pale rose, gradually changing to a lovely salmon-pink. Later it turns a beautiful brown to give a pleasant winter display. The flat flower heads will be besieged by bees.

These border perennials can be grown with the minimum of attention.

Care
Grow these late summer-/autumn-flowering sedums in well-drained soil situated in full sun. Give these plants room – about five to a square metre (square yard).

New plants
Propagate these plants by taking stem cuttings in mid-summer and rooting in sandy soil in a cold frame, or by division in late summer or autumn.

H to 60cm (24in)
S to 60cm (24in)

18–20°C
(64–68°F)

Full sun

Ornamental onion

Allium cristophii

This bulbous perennial produces ribbed stems and strap-shaped, grey-green basal leaves with stiff marginal hairs that decline as its flowers form. In early summer it bears umbels that are 25–30cm (10–12in) in diameter, and contain up to 100 star-shaped fuchsia flowers with a metallic sheen.

This plant's flower heads dry particularly well.

Care
This allium prefers full sun and humusy, well-drained soil.

New plants
Propagate from seed in spring. Remove offsets in autumn.

Giant ornamental onion

Allium giganteum

Originally from Iran, Afghanistan and Central Asia, where it grows on lower mountain slopes, this is a bulb that prefers a well-drained and sunny situation. Tall and densely flowered, it is impressive, but is not quite the giant that its name suggests. The flower stems are 1.2–1.5m (4–5ft) tall, with broad basal leaves which are withered at flowering time. The flower is a dense orb about the size of a grapefruit, formed of many purple flowers.

Care
Giant alliums like fertile, sandy to moist loam and a site in full sun or light shade.

New plants
Propagate from seed in spring. Remove offsets in autumn.

H to 30cm (12in)
S to 30cm (12in)

15–17°C (59–62°F)

Full sun

H to 1.5m (5ft)
S to 30cm (12in)

15–17°C (59–62°F)

Full sun or partial shade

Lily of the Incas, Peruvian lily

Alstroemeria aurantiaca

This tuberous-rooted plant has twisted blue-grey leaves and grows to a height of 90cm (36in). Borne on leafy stems, the flowers are trumpet-shaped in orange-red with red veins.

Plant the tubers in spring. Cover with a mulch of compost or well-rotted manure in spring. As they grow, support to prevent them being blown over. Dead-head plants to encourage more blooms. In autumn, cut stems down to the ground.

Watch for slugs and caterpillars, using an insecticide if necessary. When the plant shows yellow mottling and distorted growth, destroy it – this is a virus disease.

Care
Peruvian lilies prefer fertile, well-drained soil and a sunny, sheltered site. Avoid damaging the roots. Protect in winter.

New plants
Plant tubers 10–15cm (4–6in) deep. sow seeds in spring in a cold frame and plant out a year later. In spring the plants can be divided, but take care not to disturb the roots unduly. Sometimes the plant will not produce any stems, leaves or flowers during the first season, but once established, it can be left for years.

H to 90cm (36in)
S to 50cm (20in)

16–18°C
(61–64°F)

Full sun

Belladonna lily
Amaryllis belladonna

This bulbous plant has strap-like leaves, lasting from late winter through to mid-summer. After the leaves die down, flower stems appear and grow to a height of 75cm (30in). The trumpet-shaped fragrant pink or white flowers vary from three to twelve on a stem.

Dead-head the flowers as they fade; remove leaves and stems as they die.

Care
Belladonna lily likes a well-drained soil and a sunny, sheltered position. Keep moist when transplanting.

New plants
Plant the bulbs in summer in a warm, sheltered situation in well-drained soil. Bulbs can be divided in summer and should be replanted immediately.

H to 75cm (30in)
S to 30cm (12in)

18–20°C
(64–68°F)

Full sun

Crinum

Crinum

The large trumpet-shaped flowers of crinums bring an exotic touch to gardens in late summer and early autumn. This is a stately plant that is hardy down to around −5°C (23°F). However, to ensure that they come through cold winters, it is essential to plant crinums in a warm position – preferably at the base of a warm wall or similar protected place.

The large 15cm (6in) bulbs produce strong stems at the top of which emerge the 15cm (6in) wide, 13cm (5in) long, sweetly smelling, lily-like flowers. The six petals have a satiny look to them. Each bulb will produce three to four stems, each one bearing up to 10 flowers. Plant three or more bulbs closely together for a dramatic display. Once planted, the bulbs should be left undisturbed for several years if possible as they may take a long time to settle in again.

Care
Crinum needs a well-drained, but moisture-retentive, humus-rich soil and a sheltered, warm, sunny position.

New plants
Plants can be propagated by dividing the clumps in spring.

H to 90cm
(36in)
S to 60cm
(24in)

15–17°C
(59–62°F)

Full sun

Crocus

Crocus spp.

Crocus corms are generally known as bulbs, but they are actually solid stems from which a bud containing the leaves and flower emerges. Although regarded as spring-flowering plants, some species of crocus flower in the autumn and others in winter. So by planting a range of species you could have flowers for almost nine months!

All produce funnel-shaped, six-petalled flowers on short stems low down to the ground. The flowers, which open and close with sunlight, are available in a wide range of colours, often with a colour contrast between the inner and outer petals and often with contrasting markings. In some species the flowers open out wide but others remain goblet-shaped. Many species produce scented flowers.

The narrow, grass-like foliage usually has a central white or grey stripe and grows longer as the flowers fade. Some of the autumn-flowering species produce leaves after the flowers, but in the spring-flowering types they appear together.

Care
Crocuses grow well in any well-drained soil and prefer a site in sun or light shade. Try to keep corms dry during their summer dormancy.

New plants
Plants are propagated by removing offsets when the leaves die back.

H to 10cm
(4in)
S to 5cm (2in)

15–17°C
(59–62°F)

Full sun or
partial shade

Cyclamen
Cyclamen

The hardy cyclamen make delightful ground-cover plants under trees and shrubs and, by choosing species carefully, you can have flowers from late summer through to late spring. They are fabulous garden plants, often growing where other bulbs will not. The elegant flowers in shades of pink, crimson, mauve and white have gracefully reflexed petals and are held above the heart-shaped or rounded leaves. The latter often have fine white or silver marbling which adds to the overall attraction. Because the foliage lasts for some time it helps to sustain a long period of interest. Cyclamen are perfect for naturalising among trees and shrubs, or for growing on rock gardens and in containers.

Care
Cyclamen needs well-drained but moist, humus-rich soil and a site in partial shade. Top-dress the soil annually with leaf mould or compost and add a little bonemeal.

New plants
Unlike other plants, the tubers of cyclamen cannot be cut into sections, so the only way to increase your stock is to buy new tubers. Most species do self-seed quite reliably and dense stands of plants can be built up in this way.

H to 10cm (4in)
S to 8cm (3in)

12–18°C
(54–64°F)

Partial
shade

Winter aconite
Eranthis hyemalis

This European tuberous-rooted plant grows to a height of 10cm (4in) with a spread of 8cm (3in). The leaves are pale green and deeply cut. The bright yellow flowers appear in late winter, but in mild winters they may start blooming in mid-winter. The flowers are about 2.5cm (1in) across and look like buttercups but with a collar of pale green leaves just below the flower.

Plant tubers in a well-drained soil that is moist throughout the year – a heavy loam is ideal. Grow them in either sun or light shade. If sooty eruptions occur on the plant, destroy it to stop the spread of smut disease.

Care
Aconites prefer a well-drained, heavy soil and a site in sun or partial shade. Keep soil moist in spring.

New plants
To propagate, lift the aconites when the leaves die down. Break or cut the tubers into sections and replant these immediately, at least 8cm (3in) apart. Seed can be sown in spring and kept in a cold frame; transplant in two years and flowering will start after another year.

H to 10cm (4in)
S to 8cm (3in)

16–18°C
(61–64°F)

Full sun or
partial shade

Snowdrop
Galanthus nivalis

Snowdrop leaves are flat, sword-shaped and often blue-green in colour. The flowers are either single or double, in white with green markings on the inner petals, and can be as long as 2.5cm (1in). Snowdrops flower from mid-winter onwards. One variety of this bulbous plant flowers in late autumn, before the leaves appear. They can grow up to 20cm (8in) tall in rich soil and in partial shade.

The bulbs should be planted 10cm (4in) deep in heavy soil, or 15cm (6in) deep in light soil, in autumn. The soil should be moist but well drained. Move bulbs after they have finished flowering, while the soil is moist. Seed may take five years to bloom, so it is better to split clusters of bulbs and spread them out. Take care when lifting not to damage the roots or to let them dry out.

Care
Snowdrops like rich, well-drained soil and partial shade.

New plants
Propagate by splitting clumps and replanting as soon as flowering is over.

H to 20cm (8in)
S to 10cm (4in)

15–17°C
(59–62°F)

Partial
shade

Hyacinth
Hyacinthus spp.

Although hyacinths make excellent garden plants, they are more commonly grown indoors for winter or early spring displays on windowsills, table tops or just about anywhere else their colourful, fragrant flowers can be enjoyed.

The plants of the Dutch hyacinth *Hyacinthus orientalis* – with their erect flower heads densely packed with up to 60 flowers, and fleshy, strap-like foliage – can look perfect for up to three weeks in the right conditions. They are excellent for growing in containers outside – but ensure the compost doesn't get frosted right through – as well as in informal borders and more formal bedding schemes.

Provided the bulbs are planted in good soil with plenty of added humus they can be left in the ground all year. However, the display in the subsequent years may not be as good and when used in formal bedding schemes this may be a disadvantage. Instead, it may be a better idea to let the foliage die down, then lift the bulbs and store them in dry compost in a cool, dry place until it is time to replant in autumn.

Care
Hyacinths can be grown in any humus-rich soil. They will tolerate light shade but prefer direct sunlight.

New plants
Remove offsets in summer while the bulb is dormant.

Spring starflower
Ipheion uniflorum

These bulbous plants are noted for their grass-like, sea-green leaves and star-shaped flowers. The plants grow only 20cm (8in) tall, with spring flowers 5cm (2in) wide. The white to deep lavender-blue blooms are scented.

Bulbs should be planted in autumn. Plants should be kept weeded. When leaves and flower stems die back in summer, they should be removed. Position plants in full sun in well-drained soil. The bulbs are increased by bulblets. The plants should be lifted in autumn, divided, and replanted at once. Do this every two or three years to keep the plants free-flowering and healthy. Spring starflowers are generally trouble-free, provided the soil is kept free-draining.

Care
Spring starflowers like ordinary soil with good drainage and a site in full sun. Do not let bulbs dry out or become wet when planting or transplanting, and keep the time out of the soil to the minimum.

New plants
Propagate these flowers by dividing bulbs (including offsets) in autumn.

H to 30cm (12in)	H to 20cm (8in)
S to 10cm (4in)	S to 10cm (4in)
15–17°C (59–62°F)	15–17°C (59–62°F)
Full sun	Full sun

Iris

Iris reticulata

These hardy Asian bulbous plants have a net of fibres around the outside of the bulb and grass-like tubular leaves that are dark green with a paler tip. They are early-flowering; some start at mid-winter and others follow successively through to spring. The flowers are often 8cm (3in) wide, in lemon-yellow and blue. These plants are small and ideal for the rock garden; they rarely grow more than 15cm (6in) tall.

Plant them in a light, well-drained chalky soil. If the ground is heavy, the bulb may not flower after the first year. Give each bulb a covering of 5–8cm (2–3in) of soil. They do best when planted in autumn.

Care

Irises prefer light, well-drained, limy soil and a site in light shade or sun. Do not plant in heavy moist soil. After flowering, give a liquid feed every four weeks until the bulb dies back.

New plants

Propagate by dividing congested clumps of bulbs in the autumn.

H to 15cm (6in)
S to 5cm (2in)

18–20°C
(64–68°F)

Full sun or
partial shade

Lily
Lilium

True lilies belong to the genus *Lilium*; they include many popular species and varieties available for the garden.

The madonna lily, which has been grown in gardens for centuries, is one of the most beautiful. The simple white blooms look their best against the dark background of a hedge. Plant them among lower-growing shrubby herbs that shade the soil and keep it cool.

Lilium martagon (martagon lily or purple turk's cap) has purple flowers that give off their scent at night. This is a hardy lily that enjoys a free-draining soil with lime in full sun or partial shade. The martagon lily looks especially good growing among shrubby plants or in the shade of trees. It seeds itself freely; the bulbs should be planted deep, as this lily produces roots on its lower stem.

Care
Most lilies, with the exception of the madonna lily, enjoy deep planting. Bury the bulb up to 20cm (8in) deep. For best results the soil must be well drained so that there is no risk of waterlogging in winter. They respond to humus-rich soil and potash feed (wood ash is a good source).

New plants
Plant bulbs in the autumn; sow seeds in spring or autumn.

H to 1.8m (6ft)
S to 30cm (12in)

18–20°C
(64–68°F)

Full sun

Narcissus, Daffodil

Narcissus spp.

The genus *Narcissus* is enormous and highly varied in both size and flower form, ranging from tiny 10cm (4in) dwarf types to traditional, tall garden varieties of 60cm (24in) high. This makes daffodils indispensable and highly versatile plants.

Most daffodils flower in spring, although a few of the earlier ones will start flowering in late winter. The flower colours range from white to shades of yellow and orange-red or pink, as well as bicolours. There are singles as well as double-flowered forms.

There are choices for the rock garden, for producing informal swathes in grass and on banks, and for formal beds and borders – tall ones up to 60cm (24in) for the middle of borders, dwarf forms reaching no more than 10cm (4in) for the front – as well as for growing in containers.

To make classification of all the various species and cultivars easier, narcissi are split into 13 carefully ordered divisions.

Care

Daffodils will grow in any well-drained soil in a sunny position. However, most will tolerate light shade.

New plants

Remove offsets as the leaves die down in late spring or in early autumn as you plant the bulbs.

H to 60cm
(24in)
S to 10cm
(4in)

18–20°C
(64–68°F)

Full sun or
partial shade

Nerine

Nerine bowdenii

Nerine bowdenii, a half-hardy bulbous plant from South Africa, is sufficiently hardy to withstand most winters in the temperate zone. It will grow to a height of 60cm (24in). The blooms open in autumn, with up to eight flowers in each cluster. The clusters are 15cm (6in) across, usually rose or deep pink, but there is also a white form. The mid-green leaves are narrow and strap-like.

The bulbs should be planted in either late summer or early spring, in an ordinary well-drained soil and in a sunny position. The bulbs are placed just under the surface or, if the soil is light, they can be set deeper – as much as 10cm (4in). Where there are bulbs near the surface, they should be covered with a thick layer of bracken, leaf mould or compost to protect them against frost. They can be lifted in spring, divided and replanted to encourage larger blooms. Watch for mealy bugs and treat them with pesticide.

Care

This plant likes ordinary well-drained soil and a sunny position. Keep moist when growing.

New plants

Propagate by dividing clumps when dormant in summer.

H to 60cm
(24in)
S to 10cm
(4in)

16–18°C
(61–64°F)

Full sun

Tulip
Tulipa

Tulips are bulbous plants that are so well known that they do not need description. In addition to the many types created through selection and hybridisation, there are other species that are also worth growing. These include *Tulipa clusiana* (the lady tulip), *T. kaufmanniana* (the water-lily tulip), *T. griegii* and *T. tarda*.

Cross-bred types include Single Early and Double Early forms, which can be planted in flower borders for spring flowering. Other forms include mendels, triumph, darwins, cottage, rembrandt and parrot types.

Plant the bulbs in late autumn, in slightly alkaline soil and full sunlight. Remove the flowers after they fade, but leave the stems and leaves attached to the bulb. If the space is needed for planting summer-flowering plants, dig up the bulbs – complete with stems and leaves – and replant them into a trench in a remote position.

Care
Tulips prefer a slightly chalky soil and a site in full sunlight. Dead-head the plants to build up the bulbs for the following year.

New plants
Propagate by removing offsets in summer.

H to 60cm (24in)
S to 10cm (4in)

18–20°C
(64–68°F)

Full sun

Hart's tongue fern
Asplenium scolopendrium

This is a distinctive, evergreen, clump-forming hardy fern with leathery, bright green, strap-shaped fronds which have a heart-shaped base and a pointed tip. Grow in ordinary soil. *Asplenium scolopendrium* 'Crispum' group has boldly crimped leaves. *A. s.* 'Undulatum' group has less strong undulations.

Care
These plants can be somewhat fussy, so if they will not grow in ordinary soil, try a mix of one part peat, one part coarse sand and one part vermiculite, and make sure the mix is lime free. Always use a pot with a hole.

New plants
Propagate by division in early spring.

H to 70cm (28in)
S to 60cm (24in)

16–18°C
(61–64°F)

Partial
shade

Zebra grass
Miscanthus sinensis

This grass is a handsome, ornamental, clump-forming, herbaceous hardy perennial. It bears arching, narrow, matt to slightly bluish green leaves topped by silk-haired, greyish florets in a sheaf of slender spikes which arch with age. Grow in ordinary, ideally moist, soil in sun. Propagate by division in spring. *Miscanthus sinensis* 'Silberfeder' ('Silver Feather') is a reliable, free-flowering cultivar. *M. s.* 'Zebrinus' has broader leaves with zones of white to cream and green.

Care
This plant tolerates some drought and occasional wetness. It prefers soil that is well-drained, loamy, sandy or clay, and has an acidic to slightly alkaline pH level (6.8–7.7).

New plants
Propagation is from division and seeds in the autumn and spring. Many people prefer to cut the grass back to the ground in the spring so that new green growth is not mixed with last year's dried brown foliage.

H to 1.6m (5ft)
S to 50cm (20in)

13–16°C
(55–61°F)

Full sun

Purple moor grass

Molinia caerulea

This densely tufted, herbaceous hardy perennial has slender, arching, mid-green leaves and erect, yellow-flushed flowering stems bearing loose, narrow heads of tiny, purplish florets. Grow in moist soil in sun or partial shade. Propagate by division in spring.

Care

This grass likes well-drained to moist soil which is acid to neutral. It prefers direct sunlight but will also tolerate partial shade. Lift and divide congested clumps in autumn or spring. If it is not supported by other plants, use ring stakes or brushwood supports before flowering. Remove old flower heads in spring and comb out dead foliage using a hand fork.

New plants

Divide in spring or autumn. Sow seeds in spring in a cold frame.

H to 60cm (24in)
S to 30cm (12in)

13–16°C
(55–61°F)

Full sun or
partial shade

Fishpole bamboo, Golden bamboo
Phyllostachys aurea

This is a colourful, clump-forming hardy bamboo, with stiffly erect, grooved canes that are bright green at first, then brownish yellow. The branchlets bear narrowly lance-shaped, yellowish to golden-green leaves. Grow in ordinary soil in full sun or partial shade, sheltered from freezing winds. Propagate by division in spring. *Phyllostachys nigra*, black bamboo, has more slender green canes that turn lustrous black in their second or third year.

Care
This plant requires a good general-purpose potting soil (a soil that retains water yet drains well). Check purchased soil to see that it is well aerated and add sand or perlite and peat moss if it seems to pack too tightly.

New plants
Division of rhizomes/division in the late winter through to spring. After dividing the rhizomes, replant in the plant's regular potting mix.

H to 5m (16ft)
S to 10m (32ft)

13–16°C
(55–61°F)

Full sun or
partial shade

Common polypody
Polypodium vulgare

This is an evergreen hardy fern with narrowly triangular to lance-shaped fronds, deeply dissected into bright green lobes. Grow in well-drained soil in indirect sunlight or partial shade. *Polypodium interjectum* is very similar. 'Cornubiense' makes good ground cover.

Care
Grow in humus-rich, moist, but well-drained soil. Bright midday sun can cause damage, and this plant can be sensitive to fungicides. It is able to handle dry shade, but water regularly during the first season and mulch the tops of all containers thoroughly.

New plants
Propagate by division in spring or early summer.

H to 30cm (12in)
S to 90cm (36in)

13–16°C
(55–61°F)

Partial
shade

Holly fern, Shield fern
Polystichum setiferum

This is an evergreen, clump-forming hardy fern, with low, arching, lance-shaped fronds dissected into tiny, toothed, oval leaflets. Grow in well-drained soil in partial to full shade. Propagate by division in spring or by detaching plantlets from old fronds. 'Divisilobum' group includes cultivars with feathery, finely dissected fronds.

Care
Plant in a mostly cool, moist, lightly shaded site or full sun if given plenty of moisture. Tolerant of dry shade, but water regularly in the first season and mulch well.

New plants
Sow spores at 15–16°C (59–61°F) when ripe. Divide rhizomes in spring. Detach fronds bearing bulbils in autumn.

H to 60cm (24in)
S to 60cm (24in)

13–16°C
(55–61°F)

Partial
shade

Arrow bamboo

Pseudosasa japonica

This is a very hardy bamboo, eventually forming thickets of erect, olive-green stems which mature to pale brown. The dark green, oblong to lance-shaped leaves are 30cm (12in) or more in length. Grow in moist soil in sun or partial shade. Propagate by division or by separating rooted stems in spring.

Care

This plant requires a good genera-purpose potting soil (a soil that retains water yet drains well). Check purchased soil to see that it is well aerated and add sand or perlite and peat moss if it seems to pack too tightly.

New plants

Division in the spring. After dividing the plant, pot in the plant's regular potting mix.

H to 8m (26ft)
S to 8m (26ft)

13–16°C
(55–61°F)

Full sun or
partial shade

Palm bamboo

Sasa palmata

This is a handsome, vigorous, half-hardy bamboo which spreads widely by woody rhizomes and bears erect to slightly arching, green canes, sometimes purple-streaked. The large, broadly elliptic leaves are glossy, bright rich green with paler midribs. The leaf tips may turn brown in severe winters. Grow in ordinary, preferably moist, garden soil in sun or shade. Propagate by division or by separating rooted stems in spring. *Sasa veitchii* has scarious, parchment-coloured leaves, giving the effect of variegation.

Care

Palm bamboo requires a fertile, moisture-retentive soil that does not get waterlogged. It will grow well in most soils, including clay. If planting in free-draining soil, water well in the summer. Plant palm bamboo in full sun to part shade, away from strong winds.

New plants

Division in the spring. After dividing the plant, pot in the plant's regular potting mix.

Golden oats

Stipa arundinacea

This is an elegant, tufted, hardy evergreen, which is also known as pheasant grass, producing slender, arching, dark green leaves turning orange-brown in autumn. The large, airy, flowering plumes are formed of many purplish green florets. Grow in well-drained soil in sun. Propagate by division in spring. *Stipa calamagrostis* has bluish green leaves and smaller, more compact, floral plumes of purple-tinted to buff spikelets. *S. gigantea* is a fine, large specimen grass growing 1.8m (6ft) or more, with robust, erect stems bearing huge, loose plumes of purplish green florets which turn corn-yellow when ripe.

Care

Grow in moderately fertile, well-drained soil in full sun. Remove the old foliage in early spring.

New plants

Sow seeds in a cold frame in spring; divide from mid-spring to early summer.

H to 2.5m (8ft)
S to 6m (20ft)

16–18°C (61–64°F)

Full sun or partial shade

H to 1.8m (6ft)
S to 3m (10ft)

13–16°C (55–61°F)

Full sun

Algerian ivy, Canary Island ivy

Hedera canariensis

A vigorous, hardy, large-leaved ivy that thrives in cooler locations in a container on a sheltered patio, this is equally useful for climbing, trailing, weaving around posts or as a ground cover in a very large container. The stems and undersides of young leaves are covered with small red hairs, and until the plant reaches its adult phase – when the leaves change shape and texture – they are lobed, thick, matt and leathery. *Hedera canariensis* 'Gloire de Marengo' has leaves that are light green, edged and splashed with creamy white.

Care

Keep the compost moist during spring to autumn. In winter, apply only sufficient water to prevent it drying out. In high temperatures, increase the humidity by misting or standing the pot on a tray of moist pebbles. Feed with standard liquid fertiliser every two weeks from spring to autumn.

New plants

Adventitious roots are produced at leaf nodes along each stem, so propagation can be done by layering or by taking tip cuttings and rooting them in water or potting compost.

H to 4m (13ft)
S indefinite

16–18°C
(61–64°F)

Partial shade

Bay
Laurus nobilis

Ultimately a large evergreen shrub or small tree, this hardy, woody plant originates in the Mediterranean. It has aromatic, oval-shaped, glossy mid-green leaves and clusters of small yellow flowers that appear in spring. It can be clipped into a variety of ornamental shapes, and the dried leaves are commonly used in cooking. Although it is often grown in the garden, it also makes a good plant for a conservatory or greenhouse, especially when it is clipped into a formal shape.

Care
Keep moist in spring and summer, and spray the leaves with water occasionally to keep them clean and shining. Keep the plant out of draughts.

New plants
Take a cutting with a heel around 12cm (5in) long in early summer. Insert several cuttings in pots of seed and cutting compost, but transplant individually when the roots are established. Alternatively, layer established plants in summer.

Aeonium
Aeonium arboreum 'Zwartkop'

This is an upright, succulent, half-hardy subshrub that has long been popular in frost-free areas as a striking plant for an outdoor container. It looks equally impressive in a container on its own or used to contrast with brighter-coloured foliage or flowers. Each basal branch produces a tightly packed rosette of narrow, spoon-shaped leaves, edged with fine hairs. They are a striking dark, glossy, purple-black colour, shading to emerald green at the base, giving each rosette a green centre. Older plants will produce large, pyramid-shaped clusters of yellow flowers in spring, up to 30cm (12in) tall.

Care
Keep the compost moist at all times but not wet, and give standard liquid fertiliser once a month during the growing season. If the plant is kept in too dark a position, the leaves will become more green. In direct sunlight they may scorch. This plant must be overwintered indoors as it will not tolerate low temperatures or frost.

New plants
Take smaller rosettes as cuttings in early summer. Root in barely damp cactus compost and place in good light.

H to 12m (39ft)
S to 10m (33ft)

16–18°C (61–64°F)

Full sun

H to 90cm (36in)
S to 60cm (24in)

16–18°C (61–64°F)

Partial shade

Vegetables

Endive
Cichorium endivia

There are two types of endive: curly-leaved endive, a low-growing plant that looks a bit like curly-headed lettuce, and the broad-leaved Batavian endive, which has broader leaves and makes a more substantial and upright plant. In the kitchen endive can be used in salads – young, new leaves are best for this – or braised in butter. Traditionally, endives are blanched (grown away from light) to make them taste sweeter. Broad-leaved varieties produce attractive white leaves when blanched, although a number of varieties are self-blanching.

Sowing
Sow seed thinly in furrows 1.25cm (½in) deep and 30cm (12in) apart, from mid-spring onwards.

Cultivation
When the seedlings are 2.5cm (1in) high, thin them to 30cm (12in) apart. Once the plants reach 25cm (10in) across, place an upturned plate on the centre of each to blanch the heart. Water well in dry weather or the plants will bolt.

Harvesting
The plants will be ready to harvest about three weeks after blanching. Cut off the heads just above ground level.

H to 25cm (10in)
S to 25cm (10in)

16–18°C
(61–64°F)

Full sun

Rocket

Eruca sativa

This tender-looking plant is actually quite hardy and will survive winter temperatures down to just above freezing. The leaves have a strong, tangy flavour which increases in strength when the plant matures or is kept too dry. Rocket can be eaten raw or cooked, and grown as individual plants or harvested regularly as a cut-and-come-again crop. It makes an excellent addition to other leafy vegetables in a mixed salad.

Sowing

Sow seed in succession at three-week intervals from mid-spring to early summer. Sow in broad furrows to create a band of plants about 30cm (12in) wide. If sown in such broad furrows, weeds will be unable to establish themselves owing to the density of the plants.

Cultivation

Keep the plants well watered to promote rapid growth.

Harvesting

Either remove individual leaves from the plants, or cut the seedlings down to about 2.5cm (1in) above ground level and wait for them to resprout before cutting again.

H to 1m (3ft)
S to 25cm (10in)

16–18°C
(61–64°F)

Full sun

Lettuces

Lactuca sativa

There are many forms of this annual vegetable, grown for its fresh leaves, which are a mainstay of summer salads. For best results, grow several types, such as romaines, cabbage heads and loose-leaf lettuces. Loose-leaf types are less likely to run to seed, and are tolerant of most growing conditions. Leaf colour can vary from pale green to reddish brown, and cultivars such as 'Green Ice' and 'Red Sails' are quite deep-rooting, making them ideal for dry soils.

Sowing

Sow seed thinly in furrows 1.25cm (½in) deep and 35cm (14in) apart. Sowing at regular intervals from early spring through to mid-summer will provide a succession of lettuces from early summer through to mid-autumn.

Cultivation

When the seedlings have developed two 'true' leaves, thin to 30cm (12in) apart. In dry weather, keep the plants well watered in the last two weeks before harvesting, when they make the most growth.

Harvesting

Harvesting can begin about 12 weeks after planting. Loose-leaf lettuces should be harvested by pulling away the outer rows of leaves from one or two large plants on a regular basis. Cut off the entire heads of other types.

Cress

Lepidium sativum

Cress is a traditional sprouting crop which many people grow, often on paper, in containers on a windowsill. Cress is best grown either in spring or autumn, as it runs to seed quickly and does not relish hot weather; the plants should be kept well watered, especially in dry weather. Land, or American, cress is a good alternative to watercress and has a similar flavour. It may also be cooked. It makes a good filler for the container garden; a few seeds can be sown in situ either to grow in between other vegetables or as a border around the edge of the container.

Sowing

Sow a few seeds in situ throughout the summer. Seed sown in July and August will provide plants in the autumn.

Cultivation

Thin plants to 15cm (6in) apart.

Harvesting

Plants are ready about eight weeks after sowing. Pick leaves as required.

H to 30cm (12in)
S to 35cm (14in)

16–18°C (61–64°F)

Full sun

H to 12cm (5in)
S to 2cm (¾in)

16–18°C (61–64°F)

Full sun

Sorrel

Rumex acetosa

This versatile plant is an incredibly hardy perennial which is also very easy to grow. The tasty leaves have a sharp flavour and can be used fresh in salads or as a flavouring for soups.

Sorrel will grow on a range of soils, but prefers well-drained yet moisture-retentive, fertile conditions.

Sowing

In autumn or spring, sow seed in furrows 1.25cm (½in) deep and 30–40cm (12–16in) apart.

Cultivation

Thin the seedlings to 25–30cm (10–12in) apart. Remove any flowers or seed heads as soon as they are spotted – this will preserve the plants' energy for leaf production – and replace the plants themselves every four to five years as their productivity declines.

Harvesting

Remove the outer leaves for use as they develop, and new leaves will continue to emerge from the centre of the plant.

H to 90cm (36in)
S to 30cm (12in)

10–13°C
(50–55°F)

Full sun

Lamb's lettuce
Valeriana locusta

Also known as corn salad, this very hardy annual salad crop is grown for its mild-flavoured leaves and will survive winter temperatures down to just above freezing. The erect-growing 'French' cultivars are the hardiest; the 'Dutch' and 'English' forms have a much laxer growth habit, but are more productive. As it takes up very little room, lamb's lettuce is ideal for intercropping between slow-growing or tall vegetable crops. It will do well in most soils and is easy to grow.

Sowing
Sow seed in summer in furrows 15cm (6in) apart, with 2.5cm (1in) between the seeds. For year-round cropping, make an additional sowing in spring.

Cultivation
After germination, thin the seedlings to 10cm (4in) apart, and keep the seedbed well watered until they are about 2.5cm (1in) high.

Harvesting
Either remove individual leaves from the plants, or cut the whole head down to about 2.5cm (1in) above ground level to encourage fresh growth to be made, which can then be cut again for a further crop.

H to 30cm (12in)
S to 40cm (16in)

10–13°C
(50–55°F)

Partial
shade

Sweet peppers

Capsicum annuum 'Grossum' group

These annual plants are grown for their characteristic bell-shaped fruits. When ripe, the fruits can be red, yellow, orange and even bluish black, depending on which cultivars are grown. Sweet peppers prefer a deeply cultivated soil, but also do well in growing bags, pots and troughs; make sure the soil or potting mix is slightly acidic. They require an average temperature of around 21°C (70°F) and fairly high humidity.

Sowing
Sow seed singly in peat pots in mid-spring and germinate at 18°C (64°F). Young plants will be ready to plant out 10 weeks later.

Cultivation
Plant out 75cm (30in) apart. When the plants reach 75cm (30in) high, stake them individually and pinch back the growing point to encourage bushy growth. Spray them with water regularly to keep the humidity high. Once the fruits have started to develop, apply a high-potassium fertiliser every two weeks to encourage them to swell.

Harvesting
Pick the ripe peppers by cutting through the stalk about 2cm (¾in) from the top of the fruit.

H to 90cm (36in)
S to 30cm (12in)

18–21°C
(64–70°F)

Full sun

Chilli peppers
Capsicum frutescens

Also known as hot peppers, these plants are grown for their small, thin, tapering fruits, which are green or red when mature, depending on the cultivars grown. The flavour is often very hot, with even the mildest increasing in strength as the fruits mature. The plants can grow up to 60cm (24in) high and 45cm (18in) across, while dwarf cultivars suit pots or growing bags. Chilli and cayenne peppers require an average temperature of around 21°C (70°F) and fairly high humidity, so are often grown under protection.

Sowing
Sow seed singly in peat pots in mid-spring and germinate at 18°C (64°F).

Cultivation
Plant out 45cm (18in) apart, and when the plants reach 45cm (18in) high, pinch back the growing point to encourage bushy growth. Spray the plants with water regularly to keep the humidity high.

Harvesting
When frost is imminent, pull up the plants and hang them upside down in a frost-free place, where they will continue to ripen and can be used as needed.

H to 60cm (24in)
S to 45cm (18in)

18–21°C
(64–70°F)

Full sun

Tomatoes

Lycopersicon esculentum

Outdoor tomatoes are quite easy to grow and are among the best vegetables for the container gardener. They are attractive plants in flower and fruit. They do best in relatively warm climates, and in a sheltered position, protected by a south-facing wall. Tomatoes can be divided into two types: bush and cordon.

The cordon varieties are the most common and if they are to grow successfully, they need to be trained up a cane or tied in to wires. Tie the plants in at regular intervals, using garden string or raffia, and pinch out all the side shoots where the leaf stalks join the stem. This leaves you with one straight stem and a number of trusses of fruit. When the fourth truss has developed small tomatoes, the growing tip should be pinched out – 'stopped' – two leaves above the truss. This allows the tomatoes to develop and ripen properly. If by any chance the summer ends rather earlier than it should and you are left with a large number of green tomatoes, these can be picked and brought inside to ripen in the warmth of the house. Alternatively, you can use them to make green tomato chutney, a relish prized above many others.

Bush tomatoes are a bit simpler. These varieties grow either as small bushes, as the name implies, or trailing along the ground. They do not require either training or stopping, but you do have to cover the ground to prevent dirt or damage to the fruit; a plastic sheet is the easiest

H to 2m (80in)
S to 50cm (20in)

20–25°C
(68–77°F)

Full sun

Tomatoes (continued)
Lycopersicon esculentum

thing to use on a patio, as many of the fruits are at ground level. Dwarf tomatoes – plants that grow little more than 20cm (8in) high – are very suitable for growing in window boxes and small pots, but the yield is not large.

The flavour of tomatoes depends on the amount of sunshine they get, and the amount of watering and feeding they have received, both of which can reduce the flavour. However, all tomatoes grown in containers or growing bags need plenty of watering and feeding otherwise the yield will be minuscule.

Tomatoes prefer fertile, well-cultivated soil. They will grow successfully in pots, troughs and growing bags, but regular watering is essential to produce a good yield of large fruit.

Sowing
For outdoor cultivation, sow seed in late spring. Place individual seeds in 10cm (4in) pots and germinate at 15°C (59°F), hardening off the seedlings in a cold frame for 10 days before planting out.

Cultivation
The best growth is achieved at temperatures 20–25°C (68–77°F). The plants and fruits can be damaged when temperatures fall below 10°C (50°F), so in colder climates tomatoes are usually grown under glass or in plastic tunnels. Plant out the young plants as the first flowers open.

Tomatoes (continued)
Lycopersicon esculentum

Plant out bush types first, because they are the hardiest group. Space the plants about 90cm (36in) apart: closer spacings will produce earlier crops; wider spacings a later but heavier yield. The plants can spread along the ground, perhaps on a mulch of straw or plastic. Plant cordon types at a spacing of 75cm (30in) and train them up stakes. Remove any side shoots as they develop, so that the plant's energy goes into fruit production. As the fruits develop, apply a high-potassium fertiliser every two weeks to help them to swell. When five fruit trusses have formed, remove the main stem at two leaves above this point, to encourage even growth. Then remove the stakes and lay the plants on straw to encourage quicker ripening.

To extend the growing season, plastic tunnels can be used to protect the crops.

Harvesting
Cropping usually starts within 10 weeks of transplanting. Pick the fruits as they ripen and remove any leaves covering the fruit to encourage more to do so. If frost threatens in autumn, uproot the plants and hang up in a dry, frost-free place to allow the remaining fruits to ripen.

Aubergines
Solanum melongena

The aubergine is grown for its egg-shaped fruits, which are usually a blackish purple but may be white-flushed or completely white in cultivars such as 'Easter Egg'. The plants can reach 75cm (30in) high and 60cm (24in) across, and have a deep root system. They therefore prefer a deep, fertile soil, but will also grow well in containers if fertilised and watered generously. Grow in a warm, sheltered spot.

Sowing
Sow seed in small pots in mid-spring and germinate at 25°C (77°F). After germination, you will need to lower the temperature to about 16°C (61°F) – if higher than this, the plants will become spindly and prone to collapse.

Cultivation
Plant out as the first flowers start to open, but after there is little risk of frost. Space the plants 75cm (30in) apart, and stake them individually to provide extra support. When the main stem reaches 45cm (18in) high, pinch back the growing point to encourage bushy growth. Once the fruits have started to develop, apply a high-potassium fertiliser every two weeks to help them to swell.

Harvesting
Pick the fruits when they are fully swollen, shiny, and firm with a smooth skin. If left too long before picking, the flesh will become bitter.

H to 75cm (30in)
S to 60cm (24in)

16–25°C
(61–77°F)

Full sun

Cucumber
Cucumis sativus

These tender plants are grown for their characteristic fruits with a high water content. Some cultivars have a bushy, compact habit while others can trail over several metres.

Cucumbers will not tolerate temperatures below 10°C (50°F), so a frost-free environment is essential. The plants will do well in soilless potting mix in growing bags.

Sowing
In mid-spring, sow seeds two to a 8cm (3in) pot in a temperature of 18–30°C (64–86°F). Thin to one seed per pot.

Cultivation
Once there is little risk of frost and the seedlings are 30cm (12in) high, gradually harden off those to be grown outside. Plant at least 40–45cm (16–18in) apart, with 90cm (36in) between rows, to allow lots of light to reach the plants. Train trailing types vertically as cordons up nets or strings at least 1.8m (6ft) high. Twist support strings around the plants to hold them upright.

Harvesting
The fruits will be ready to harvest by late summer, about eight weeks after sowing. Cut them from the plant, leaving a stalk of about 2.5cm (1in) on each fruit.

H to 2.5m (8ft)
S to 45cm (18in)

16–18°C (61–64°F)

Full sun

Globe artichokes
Cynara cardunculus 'Scolymus' group

These large, bushy perennials are grown for their greenish purple flower bracts and have a cropping life of three years.

Sowing
Sow seed 2.5cm (1in) deep in a seedbed in early spring in rows 30cm (12in) apart with 10cm (4in) between the seeds. Transplant into the cropping site in early summer. These seedlings will be variable, however, so division of named varieties is preferable.

Cultivation
Before planting, spread a 10cm (4in) layer of well-rotted manure and dig the ground to one spade's depth. Plant young side shoots 5cm (2in) deep and 90cm (36in) apart all around, and trim back the shoots by half their length to prevent wilting. After planting, spread a 10cm (4in) layer of manure around the plants to reduce weeds and moisture loss. Protect over winter with a layer of straw, until early spring, when each plant will produce two or three shoots to bear the flower heads.

Harvesting
From early summer to early autumn, depending on the age of the plants, each stem will carry one primary flower head and several secondary ones. These should be cut when they are about 10cm (4in) across, removing each one with a 10cm (4in) section of stem.

H to 2.5m (8ft)
S to 75cm (30in)

16–25°C
(61–77°F)

Full sun

Courgettes and marrows
Cucurbita pepo

Another member of the cucumber family, courgettes are a widely grown favourite summer vegetable. Those grown in the garden are far better to eat than any bought in a shop. The best courgettes to grow are the compact bush varieties; provided the fruits are harvested regularly, they will continue to produce fruit over a long period.

Grown for their long, cylindrical fruits, courgettes come in a range of colours from white, through grey, to deep green; some cultivars, such as 'Spineless Beauty', are a mixture of green and cream-white stripes. The fruits, with their smooth, shiny skin, will be ready to harvest about six to eight weeks after sowing.

Although any variety of these immature squashes can be eaten when young, it is best to choose a modern hybrid variety of courgette. Numerous new cultivars have been introduced, with fruit colours ranging from the dark green of 'Embassy', through lighter shades, to the yellow of 'Gold Rush'.

Sowing
In spring, soak the seeds overnight and then sow individually in 8cm (3in) peat pots at a temperature of 15°C (59°F).

H to 90cm (36in)
S to 1.2m (4ft)

16–18°C
(61–64°F)

Full sun

Courgettes and marrows (continued)
Cucurbita pepo

Cultivation

Harden off the young plants before planting out. Plant bush types 90cm (36in) apart; trailing cultivars will need at least 1.2m (4ft) all around unless trained vertically, when they can be planted at the same spacing as bush types. Immediately after planting out, make sure that the plants are protected from overnight frost.

Each plant needs a minimum of 13.5 litres (3 gallons) of water per week. Mulch with a layer of organic matter at least 10cm (4in) deep, to retain soil moisture. Cut away any leaves shading the fruits. As the fruits start to swell, remove any male flowers close by to prevent the fruits developing a bitter taste.

Harvesting

Although they can grow much larger, courgettes are usually harvested when the fruits are 10–15cm (4–6in) long. Regular picking encourages the production of further flowers and fruits. Towards the end of the season, allow one or two fruits to mature into marrows. These can then be stored for several months in an airy, frost-free environment. Remember to avoid leaving marrows too long or they will become tough. Pick when the fruits are 25cm (10in) long – if your thumbnail goes in easily, they are ready.

Squashes and pumpkins

Cucurbita maxima, C. moschata

Pumpkins belong to the same family as marrows and courgettes, and come in a wide range of shapes, sizes and colours. They are not suitable for a patio garden with limited room, but there is no doubt that a traditional orange pumpkin is a triumph for the gardener at Hallowe'en.

These tender plants are grown for their unusual fruits, which vary tremendously in shape and size – from the large, orange fruits of the traditional Hallowe'en pumpkin to the curved shape of crookneck and the distinctive 'Turk's Turban' squash. They can weigh up to 227kg (500lb) each and come in a range of colours from yellow to grey-green.

Squashes, crooknecks and pumpkins grow best in a warm, sheltered position and are generally ready to harvest seven weeks after sowing. 'Gold Bar' is a useful cultivar, producing fruits weighing up to 1kg (2¼lb). 'Park's' crookneck has fewer spines so is less prickly to harvest.

Sowing
In mid- to late spring, soak the seeds overnight in cold water and then sow individually in 8cm (3in) pots. Raise at 12–14°C (54–57°F).

Cultivation
Harden off the young plants for two to three weeks before planting out once there is little risk of frost. However, if frost is forecast, make sure that the plants are protected

H to 60cm (24in)
S to 1m (3ft)

12–14°C
(54–57°F)

Partial
shade

Squashes and pumpkins (continued)
Cucurbita maxima, C. moschata

with fleece. Plant bush types 90cm (36in) apart; trailing cultivars need at least 1.2m (4ft) all around.

Each plant requires a minimum of 13.5 litres (3 gallons) of water per week. Mulch with a layer of organic matter at least 10cm (4in) deep, to retain soil moisture. Cut away any leaves that shade the fruits. As the fruits start to swell, remove any male flowers that are close by to prevent the fruits developing a bitter taste.

Harvesting
Although they can grow much larger, the fruits are usually harvested when 20–25cm (8–10in) across, or when the foliage starts to turn yellow and the fruit stems start to crack. This is often just before the first hard frost occurs. After severing the fruit from the parent plant, dry it for about 10 days outdoors, using the warmth of the sun to improve storage quality. Then place the fruit in a string or netting bag, and hang it in an airy, frost-free place at a temperature of 10°C (50°F) for up to six months.

Protecting seedlings
Inverted jam jars can be used to protect young plants.

Ripening pumpkins
Lay black plastic sheeting underneath ripening pumpkins, crooknecks and other squashes to keep them off the ground.

Sweetcorn

Zea mays

Sweetcorn is the modern descendant of a very ancient plant native to Central America. Not surprisingly, it is more at home in a Mediterranean climate than in a cool temperate one, but given purpose-bred varieties and a good summer, there is every chance of success in reasonably mild regions. The site should be open and must receive plenty of sun. A soil well supplied with garden compost or manure and sufficient lime to correct strong acidity is also necessary. In order to get good results, sweetcorn must have a long growing season. Modern varieties will be ready for picking about four months after sowing. However, you must balance this

with having the plants inside and protected while there is still a risk of spring frosts. Sow the seeds, therefore, in a greenhouse in mid-spring or in a cold frame from mid- to late spring. Plant the seedlings out when the risk of frost is over. If you do not have either a greenhouse or cold frame, you can sow the seeds where the plants are to grow outdoors in late spring or early summer.

Once established, keep weeds at bay to avoid competition. When hoeing, be careful not to disturb, and certainly not damage, the surface roots; these are important feeding roots as well as the plant's main support. Provide plenty of water in dry weather. Do not

H to 2.5m (8ft)
S to 30cm (12in)

16–25°C
(61–77°F)

Full sun

Sweetcorn (continued)
Zea mays

plant traditional and supersweet varieties together, as cross-pollination can affect the quality of the supersweets.

Sowing
Sow seed under protection, with three seeds to an 8cm (3in) pot. Outdoors, sow seed from mid-spring in a seedbed in a warm, sheltered spot.

Cultivation
Sweetcorn relies on the wind to pollinate the plants. To facilitate this, plant in square or rectangular, six-row blocks, with the plants spaced 35cm (14in) apart all around.

Before transplanting pot-grown seedlings, cover the planting area with black plastic to warm the soil. When the seedlings are 15–20cm (6–8in) high, insert the young plants into the soil through the plastic and shelter them from wind for the first week after planting. Most of the plants will produce four or five cobs – to get large cobs, water the plants well as the cobs are developing.

Harvesting
The cobs will be ready to harvest from mid-summer to mid-autumn. When the tassel ('silk') at the top of the cob starts to turn brown, snap the cob from the main stem.

Okra

Abelmoschus esculentus

Grown for its elegant, edible pods, okra is nicknamed lady's finger because of its resemblance in shape. This tender vegetable must have as long a growing season as possible, because it will take at least seven weeks from sowing until harvesting the pods.

Sowing
In mid-spring, sow three seeds per 8cm (3in) pot at a temperature of 18–24°C (64–75°F). Thin the two smallest seedlings from each pot.

Cultivation
The plants should be 15–20cm (6–8in) high before they are planted out, usually from early summer onwards, once there is little risk of frost. Before planting, cover the planting area with black plastic for at least three weeks to warm the soil, and insert the young plants into the soil through the plastic. Space them at 35cm (14in) all around to encourage strong, bushy plants. They must be sheltered from winds for the first week after being planted.

Harvesting
From mid-summer until early autumn, harvest the pods while they are still immature and before the seeds have developed fully. Cut them from the stem with a sharp knife. Harvest the pods as they form, to encourage the plant to produce more.

S to 90cm (36in)
S to 60cm (24in)

18–24°C
(64–75°F)

Full sun

Peas

Pisum sativum

Garden peas are grown for their sweet-tasting, edible seeds, which are produced in green or (in a few cultivars) purple pods. The peas are generally round with a wrinkled or smooth skin, and can be eaten fresh – either cooked, or raw in salads – or dried and stored for use later.

   The time from sowing to harvesting varies with each type. If you sow early-crop peas in mid-spring, they will be ready to harvest 12 weeks later in mid-summer. Crops of maincrop cultivars will be ready to harvest about 10–12 weeks after sowing.

Sowing

Sow seed in flat-bottomed furrows 2.5–5cm (1–2in) deep. String foil across the rows to deter birds from taking the seeds or attacking the seedlings.

Cultivation

Keep the plants well watered from soon after flowering starts.

Harvesting

Start harvesting the pods when they are well developed but before they become too tightly packed with peas. Keep picking regularly to encourage further flowering.

H to 1.5m (5ft)
S to 50cm (20in)

16–18°C
(61–64°F)

Partial
shade

Mangetouts

Pisum sativum var. macrocarpon

Also known as snow peas, mangetouts are grown for their delicate, sweet-tasting pods, which are eaten young and whole. Alternatively, mangetouts can be harvested later, in the same way as garden peas.

Sowing

Sow seeds from mid-spring onwards at three-week intervals to provide a succession of crops throughout the summer. Sow in flat-bottomed furrows 4cm (1½in) wide and 15cm (6in) apart, with 10cm (4in) between the seeds. For cropping purposes, sow in blocks of three furrows, which can be separated from the next block by a 45cm (18in) path.

Cultivation

The crop is larger when the plants are supported by stakes, sticks, or plastic or wire mesh. With the three-row system, arrange the support over the rows in a tent-like structure, about 45–60cm (18–24in) tall.

Harvesting

The perfect stage for picking is eight weeks after sowing, when the peas are just visibly swelling in the pods. Harvest the pods by tugging them gently from the stem.

Scarlet runners

Phaseolus coccineus

These easy-to-grow vines were originally introduced as ornamentals. Today, scarlet runners are grown mainly for their long, edible pods, which are produced prolifically until the first frost.

Grown as annuals, scarlet runners require a sturdy support system, because they can reach heights of 2.5–3m (8–10ft) in their growing season of 10 weeks.

Sowing

Sow seeds in late spring or early summer – scarlet runners grow better in warm soil. Using a dibber, spot-sow 5cm (2in) deep in two rows spaced 60cm (24in) apart and with 15cm (6in) between the seeds, to give the plants plenty of room as they grow. In colder areas, sow the beans indoors, two or three to a 15cm (6in) pot. Transplant when about 10cm (4in) tall.

Cultivation

Insert the supports when the plants are about 15cm (6in) high, just as the twining stem starts to develop in the tip of the plant. Water the roots well from soon after flowering and continue throughout the harvesting period.

Harvesting

The pods will be ready for picking from mid-summer onwards and harvesting can continue until the first frost, when the plants are killed.

H to 1.8m (6ft)
S to 50cm (20in)

13–18°C (55–64°F)

Partial shade

H to 3m (10ft)
S to 60cm (24in)

16–18°C (61–64°F)

Full sun

Butter beans

Phaseolus lunatus

Also known as the lima bean, this plant is grown for its large, white seeds, although the young pods can be eaten whole about six weeks after sowing. The plants prefer a warm climate and a well-drained soil.

There are both bush and pole forms of the lima bean – the latter being useful in small gardens where space is at a premium.

Sowing

Sow seeds from late spring onwards 8cm (3in) deep and 30–45cm (12–18in) apart. Allow 75cm (30in) between the rows for pole cultivars, and slightly less for bush forms.

Cultivation

Provide pole cultivars with stakes at least 1.8m (6ft) tall for adequate support. Once the plants reach 30cm (12in) high, supply a brand-name liquid fertiliser at two-week intervals to ensure growth, but stop fertilising when the plants start to flower.

Harvesting

The beans will be ready to harvest 10 weeks after sowing, when the swollen seeds are visible in the pods. Pull pods gently to prevent damage to the stems.

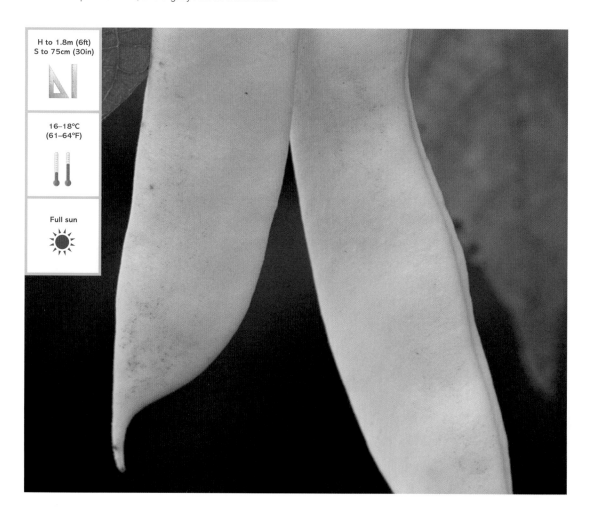

H to 1.8m (6ft)
S to 75cm (30in)

16–18°C
(61–64°F)

Full sun

French beans

Phaseolus vulgaris

Also known as green beans, French beans are grown for their curved, green pods, which are eaten whole, and for their partially developed seeds. Bush forms will grow 40–45cm (16–18in) high and 30–45cm (12–18in) wide. Pole cultivars can be grown up supports.

Sowing
Sow seeds at three-week intervals from late spring until mid-summer. Plant 5cm (2in) deep in two rows spaced 20cm (8in) apart, with about 15cm (6in) between seeds. Stagger them to give plenty of room.

Cultivation
Keep plants well watered once flowering starts, to increase the crop and delay the onset of stringiness.

Harvesting
The beans should be ready to harvest eight weeks after sowing. Pick regularly once the pods are about 10cm (4in) long and will snap cleanly in half.

Weather protection
A late crop of green beans should be protected by glass.

H to 45cm (18in)
S to 45cm (18in)

16–18°C
(61–64°F)

Partial
shade

Asparagus peas
Psophocarpus tetragonolobus

Asparagus peas are grown for their decorative, scarlet to chocolate-brown flowers, delicate bluish green foliage, and triangular, winged pods that have an asparagus-like flavour. They are eaten whole. These plants grow best in a sunny position in a well-drained soil.

Sowing
Sow seeds in mid- to late spring, in furrows about 2.5cm (1in) deep and 30cm (12in) apart, with about 30cm (12in) between the seeds.

Cultivation
Support the plants with stakes, sticks or plastic or wire mesh, otherwise they will produce very few pods. Protection from birds is essential: suspending nets on stakes above the crop is the best method.

Harvesting
The pods will be ready for picking about eight weeks after sowing, from mid-summer until early autumn. For the best flavour, harvest the pods while still immature and 2.5–5cm (1–2in) long. Pick regularly to encourage further flowering and the production of more pods. However, do not expect large quantities of pods: even a heavy yield will be only about half that of garden peas.

Broad beans
Vicia faba

Broad beans are very hardy plants, and will give a good crop with very little care and attention. They are grown mainly for their edible, greenish white seeds, which develop inside thick, hairy pods, but the immature pods can be eaten when about 10cm (4in) long and the young shoots are also tasty. Those sown in autumn will take up to 20 weeks to harvest; spring-sown crops are ready in 12 weeks.

Sowing
Seeds germinate better at lower temperature, so sow in late autumn (this will discourage aphids, to which broad beans are prone, since the plants will flower before the aphids are out in force) or in early spring. Using a dibber, spot-sow 5cm (2in) deep in two rows spaced at 30cm (12in) apart, with 25cm (10in) between the seeds to give plenty of room.

Cultivation
Most cultivars need support, and well-branched twigs 45cm (18in) tall will allow the plants to grow up through them. Water the plants well when flowering starts and throughout harvest-time.

Harvesting
If you sow in autumn and spring, you should have broad beans for picking from late spring to mid-autumn.

H to 45cm (18in)
S to 60cm (24in)

16–18°C (61–64°F)

Full sun

H to 90cm (36in)
S to 45 cm (18in)

16–18°C (61–64°F)

Partial shade

Swiss chard

Beta vulgaris 'Cicla' group

This hardy vegetable is grown for its large, glossy, succulent leaves, which can be up to 45cm (18in) long and 20cm (8in) wide. The brightly coloured leaf stalks are red or white, and the leaves range in colour from the deep green of 'Fordhook Giant' to the lime-green of 'Lucullus' or copper-green of 'Rhubarb Chard'. The best known is red-stemmed Swiss chard, also known as ruby chard, which is easy to grow but prone to bolting, especially in hot, dry weather. Swiss chard prefers a fertile, well-drained but moisture-retentive soil.

Sowing

Incorporate plenty of organic matter into the soil before sowing. Sow seed for new plants at any time from early spring to mid-summer into furrows 2cm (¾in) deep and 45cm (18in) apart, with 15cm (6in) between the seeds.

Cultivation

When the seedlings are about 5cm (2in) high, thin them to 30cm (12in) apart – as a long-term crop, the plants need plenty of room or mildew may attack them. For cut-and-come-again crops, thin to 8cm (3in) apart.

Harvesting

Harvest the plants grown at wider spacings by cutting off the outer leaves at soil level.

H to 60cm (24in)
S to 45cm (18in)

16–18°C
(61–64°F)

Full sun

Cabbages
Brassica oleracea 'Capitata' group

The tightly packed leaves and growing point of the cabbage plant are often referred to as the 'head' or 'heart', and this varies in size and shape – from round, through pointed, to almost flat – according to type and cultivar. Growing a selection of the many types on offer makes it possible to have fresh cabbage available to eat year-round, harvesting even through quite severe winter conditions.

All types of cabbage are cultivated in much the same way, with the timing of sowing and planting varying according to the season, the cultivars chosen, and the time taken to reach maturity. The soil should be slightly alkaline to discourage a disease called club root, so apply lime if necessary.

Sowing
Sow seed thinly 2cm (¾in) deep in a well-prepared seedbed outdoors from mid- to late spring through to mid-summer, depending on the cabbage type. For many of the sowings, watering may be required to make sure the seedlings keep growing rapidly. If cabbages dry out, they will produce hearts too easily or bolt to produce seed.

How to transplant brassicas
When the seedlings have three or four 'true' leaves, they are ready for transplanting into rows 30cm (12in) apart, with 45cm (18in) between the plants.

H to 45cm(18in)
S to 45cm (18in)

16–18°C
(61–64°F)

Full sun

Cabbages (continued)

Brassica oleracea 'Capitata' group

This crop matures quite rapidly and can take as little as 10 weeks from germination to harvest. However, because it is shallow-rooted it is very important to keep the plants well watered.

Before transplanting, check that the growing point on a young plant is undamaged. Embed the seedlings to the depth of the lowest 'true' leaves to stabilise the plants. The plant is firmly enough planted only if a leaf snaps or tears when tugged.

Cultivation

Transplant the seedlings. Firm the soil well by treading it down before planting, to encourage a strong root system that will support the plants. Plant out spring cabbages at a spacing of 30cm (12in) all around, summer and autumn types at 40 x 45cm (16 x 18in), and hardy winter cabbages at a spacing of 50 x 50cm (20 x 20in) apart.

Harvesting

When the cabbage has developed a good-sized, solid heart, it is ready for harvesting. Using a sharp knife, cut through the main stem to remove the entire heart and a few outer leaves, leaving the oldest leaves and the stem in the soil.

Brussels sprouts

Brassica oleracea 'Gemmifera' group

These very hardy vegetables are grown for their edible flower buds, which form small, tight, cabbage-like sprouts in the leaf joints of the plant's main stem. Tall cultivars are ideal if space is limited, since they can be grown close together and produce a good 'vertical' crop. The soil for Brussels sprouts should be slightly alkaline to discourage club root disease, so apply lime if necessary. They take about 12 weeks from sowing to harvesting.

Sowing

Sow seed thinly into a seedbed outdoors in mid- to late spring. Some watering may be required to make sure that the seedlings keep growing rapidly.

Cultivation

Firm the soil well by treading it down before planting, to encourage a strong root system that will hold the plants erect. When the seedlings have developed three or four 'true' leaves, transplant them into their cropping site with the rows 60cm (24in) apart and 60cm (24in) between the plants, firming each plant well into the soil.

Harvesting

The sprouts will be ready to harvest from early autumn through to mid-spring, depending on the cultivar. To pick, pull the individual sprouts downwards so that they snap from the stem.

H to 1m (3ft)
S to 60cm (24in)

15–18°C
(59–64°F)

Full sun

Kale
Brassica oleracea 'Acephala' group

This is the hardiest of annual winter vegetables. The soil for kale should be slightly alkaline to discourage club root disease, so apply lime if necessary.

Sowing
Sow seed in late spring outdoors in a seedbed. You may need to protect the seedlings against birds.

Cultivation
When the seedlings have developed four 'true' leaves, transplant them into their cropping site, spacing the rows about 60cm (24in) apart, with 45cm (18in) between the plants. Water well until established.

Harvesting
Harvest on a cut-and-come-again basis from mid-autumn to mid-spring by snapping off young leaves from all the plants. This will prevent any leaves maturing and becoming tough and stringy.

Hoeing between rows
Hoeing between kale plants controls weeds as they emerge.

Chinese cabbage
Brassica rapa 'Chinensis' group

This annual plant is grown for its crisp, delicately flavoured leaves with white midribs, which are used fresh in salads. It is relatively fast-growing and may be ready to harvest as little as eight weeks from germination.

Chinese cabbage resents root disturbance and is usually raised in pots. Transplant seedlings when three 'true' leaves are about 5cm (2in) high.

Sowing
Sow seed individually in plastic or peat pots 8cm (3in) square in mid-summer. They need temperatures of 20–25°C (68–77°F) to germinate, so raise in a cold frame or greenhouse.

Cultivation
When the seedlings have developed four 'true' leaves, transplant outdoors into rows about 30cm (12in) apart, with 45cm (18in) between the plants. Chinese cabbage is shallow-rooted, and the plants must be kept well watered.

Harvesting
Starting in late summer, harvesting can last for up to 14 weeks with successional sowings. Cut through the stem just above ground level to remove the heart. The remaining stalk will often sprout clusters of new leaves, which can be harvested later on.

H to 60cm (24in)
S to 60cm (24in)

10–13°C (50–55°F)

Partial shade

H to 45cm (18in)
S to 30cm (12in)

20–25°C (68–77°F)

Full sun

Purple sprouting broccoli
Brassica oleracea 'Italica' group

Grown for its edible flower heads, which are harvested while in tight bud, purple sprouting broccoli is a very hardy, biennial, winter vegetable. There are both white- and purple-flowered forms. The soil for broccoli should be slightly alkaline in order to discourage club root disease, so apply lime if necessary.

Sowing
Sow seeds individually in 5cm (2in) square plastic or peat pots, in a cold frame or unheated greenhouse in spring.

Cultivation
Plant out in early summer with 60cm (24in) between the plants all around. Water is essential to produce a good crop, the critical time being the first month after sowing. Surround young stems with extra soil to reduce windrock.

Harvesting
Broccoli can be harvested from late winter until late spring and has a natural cut-and-come-again habit. Cut the central spike first, before the flowers start to open; side shoots will also try to flower and these smaller spikes can be cut later.

H to 60cm (24in)
S to 30cm (12in)

16–18°C (61–64°F)

Full sun

Cauliflowers

Brassica oleracea 'Botrytis' group

Cauliflowers are grown for their edible flower heads, which are harvested while they are in tight bud. Cauliflowers can be available for most of the year, and certainly from early spring through to mid-winter. Autumn- and spring-heading cauliflowers are the easiest to grow, often producing curds (immature flower heads) up to 30cm (12in) across. They will be ready to harvest in 8–10 weeks.

Cauliflowers are often judged on the whiteness of their curds and the lack of blemishes on them. There are also forms with green and purple heads, which have an outstanding flavour.

Cauliflowers are among the most difficult vegetables to grow well. They need plenty of water to ensure rapid growth and they resent root disturbance, so should be transplanted as young as possible, certainly within six weeks of germination. If transplanted too late or allowed to dry out at this stage, they may produce small, premature, tight curds that are tough and woody.

The soil for cauliflowers should be slightly alkaline to discourage club root disease and because acidic soils can promote some nutrient deficiencies, resulting in poor curds. Apply lime if necessary.

Sowing

Sow seeds individually in plastic or peat pots 8cm (3in) square, and raise in a cold frame or unheated greenhouse.

H to 60cm (24in)
S to 60cm (24in)

16–18°C
(61–64°F)

Full sun

Cauliflowers (continued)

Brassica oleracea 'Botrytis' group

Sow early-summer cauliflowers in mid-autumn for harvesting the following spring; autumn cauliflowers in late spring for harvesting in autumn; winter cauliflowers in late spring for harvesting the following winter; and sow spring cauliflowers in late spring for harvesting in early spring the following year.

Cultivation

When the seedlings have developed four 'true' leaves, they are ready for transplanting to their cropping site. Spacing depends on the time of year; generally, the later the planting, the larger the cauliflower will grow and the greater the space needed for each plant. Early-summer cauliflowers, for example, should be planted at a spacing of 60 x 45cm (24 x 18in) and winter cauliflowers at 75cm (30in) all around.

Harvesting

When the covering leaves start to open and show the enclosed curd beneath, the cauliflower is ready to harvest. Using a sharp knife, cut through the main stem to remove the complete curd, together with a row of leaves around it to protect the curd from damage and marking.

Broccoli/Calabrese

Brassica oleracea 'Italica' group

Grown as an annual for its edible flower heads, broccoli (also called calabrese) is similar to sprouting broccoli but less hardy, although it can be harvested in early spring if grown under protection. Many cultivars will mature within eight weeks of sowing.

Well-grown broccoli is tasty eaten fresh and ideal for freezing, the drawback being that the plant is very susceptible to mealy aphids, attracted to the flower spikes.

The soil for broccoli should be slightly alkaline in order to discourage club root disease, so apply lime if necessary. Broccoli resents root disturbance and often responds to transplanting by prematurely producing small, tight heads that can be tough and woody.

Sowing

Sow seed thinly in furrows 2.5cm (1in) deep and about 30cm (12in) apart, sowing three seeds 1.25cm (½in) apart in spots at 20cm (8in) intervals. Alternatively, sow seeds individually into 5cm (2in) diameter plastic or peat pots in a cold frame or unheated greenhouse if cold weather demands an earlier start.

Cultivation

When the seedlings have developed three 'true' leaves, thin them to leave only the strongest and healthiest seedling at each spot. Transplant pot-grown seedlings at this point. Watering is essential to keep the plants growing rapidly and to produce a good crop – critical times are the first month after sowing and the three-week period just before cropping commences.

Harvesting

The main cropping season is from early summer to mid-autumn, but harvesting can continue until the plants are damaged by the first frost, before the flowers (usually yellow) start to open. The slightly smaller spikes produced by the side shoots can be cut later. Main-season plantings will often yield up to four or five cuttings before the plants are discarded. (They make useful compost.)

Applying lime

Lime can be applied at any time of year to raise the soil's pH but must be added alone, at least two to three months after manuring, or one month after fertilising the soil. This is because lime and nitrogen react to release ammonia, which can harm plants.

If lime is used first, however, fertilisers and manures can be added just one month later. It is also simpler to add lime before crops are sown or transplanted into the site. If lime is applied too often, plants may show signs of nutrient deficiency. Bear in mind that it is easier to raise the soil pH than it is to lower it.

H to 60cm (24in)
S to 30cm (12in)

16–18°C (61–64°F)

Full sun

Pak choi

Brassica rapa var. *chinensis*

Closely related to the Chinese cabbage, all parts of the pak choi plant can be eaten. Varieties differ in height from 8–10cm (3–4in) to 45cm (18in). Look for bolt-resistant varieties.

Sowing
Sow seeds in situ 1.25cm (½in) deep, in rows 30cm (12in) apart, every few weeks for a continuous crop. Thin according to the size desired: small, 15cm (6in) apart; medium, 18cm (7in) apart; large, 35cm (14in) apart. Sow under cover in autumn for a winter crop.

Cultivation
Keep weed-free and water well.

Harvesting
Ready in three weeks. Pick the leaves as needed, leaving the plant in the ground to resprout.

Spinach

Spinacia oleracea

This reasonably hardy vegetable is renowned for its strongly flavoured, dark green leaves, which are rich in iron and vitamins.

Spinach prefers a well-drained but moisture-retentive, fertile soil that is high in nitrogen. It will tolerate light shade. Although a perennial, it is best grown as an annual in order to produce the most vigorous leaves. The plants will often bolt (run to seed) and develop seed in the first year, especially during periods of hot, dry weather.

Sowing
For a continuous supply, sow seed thinly in furrows at three-week intervals from early spring to mid-summer.

Cultivation
When the seedlings are 2.5cm (1in) high, thin them to 15cm (6in) apart. For cut-and-come-again crops, thin to 5cm (2in).

Harvesting
Spinach is usually ready for eating about six weeks after sowing. Individual leaves can be removed, or the whole plant cut back to produce new leaves for cut-and-come-again harvesting. Harvest plants grown at wide spacings by cutting off the outer leaves at ground level.

H to 45cm (18in)
S to 35cm (13in)

20–25°C (68–77°F)

Full sun

H to 30cm (12in)
S to 40cm (16in)

16–18°C (61–64°F)

Full sun

Leeks
Allium porrum

Like onions, you can sow leeks either in a heated greenhouse in mid- to late winter or outside in the early to mid-spring. In either event, plant the seedlings outside in their final position when they are about as thick as pencils.

To grow leeks, plant out the seedlings in early to mid-summer. Make holes 15cm (6in) deep and 15cm (6in) apart and, having trimmed the roots back to about 1.25cm (½in) long, drop a plant into each hole. No firming in is needed; you merely pour water into the hole. This covers the roots with soil and ensures that the little plants will flourish.

One of the hardiest of winter vegetables, leeks have a long cropping season, from early autumn, through winter, and into late spring of the following year.

Sowing
In late spring, sow seeds thinly, 2.5cm (1in) apart, in drills 2.5cm (1in) deep and 30cm (12in) apart.

Cultivation
Transplant seedlings when they are 20cm (8in) high, the main planting season being mid-summer. Incorporate a dressing of high-nitrogen fertiliser into the soil surface before planting.

Harvesting
Harvest leeks when their leaves start to hang down, from early autumn onwards, by lifting them with a garden fork.

H to 60cm (24in)
S to 20cm (8in)

16–18°C
(61–64°F)

Full sun

Celeriac

Apium graveolens 'Rapaceum' group

This vegetable is grown for its celery-flavoured, swollen stem, which takes six months to mature after sowing. It can be cooked or used raw.

Grow celeriac in a sunny, open site in free-draining soil. It may eventually reach 75cm (30in) high.

Sowing

Sow seed in trays or modules under protection, at a temperature of 16°C (61°F), from early spring onwards for a continuous supply.

Cultivation

About six weeks after sowing, harden off the seedlings in a cold frame. Plant them out in rows 30cm (12in) apart, with 40cm (16in) between the plants, with the stems just visible on the soil surface. In late autumn, remove the outer leaves to encourage the stems to swell, and mulch with straw to protect from severe frost.

Harvesting

Harvest celeriac from late summer until the following spring, digging up the plants with a garden fork. However, plants will survive in the ground in most sites.

Asparagus

Asparagus officinalis

This herbaceous perennial can produce crops of its delicious shoots (spears) for up to 25 years, so requires a permanent site.

Asparagus prefers deep, fertile, well-drained soil that has had plenty of organic matter incorporated into it two to three months before planting. In spring, before the spears emerge, the soil is often top-dressed with salt, which controls weeds but does not harm the crop.

Cultivation

Asparagus plants grown from seed give a variable crop, so it is best to purchase one-year-old asparagus crowns. Plant these in early spring, 10–15cm (4–6in) deep and 45cm (18in) apart, in ridge-bottomed trenches 30cm (12in) apart. Cut down and remove all top-growth in late autumn as it turns yellow.

Harvesting

After the asparagus bed has been established for one to two years, you can then harvest the spears. Harvesting usually begins in mid-spring and lasts for eight weeks. When the spears are 15cm (6in) high, cut them with a sharp knife, slicing through the stem 2–3cm (1¾–1¼in) below soil level. Keep the cut spears covered to prevent them drying out.

H to 60cm (24in)
S to 30cm (12in)

16–18°C (61–64°F)

Full sun

H to 1.5m (5ft)
S to 90cm (36in)

16–18°C (61–64°F)

Full sun

Celery
Apium graveolens

Celery is grown for its crisp, blanched leaf stalks, which can be white, pink or red. Newer, self-blanching forms are easier to grow, since they do not need to be artificially blanched. Celery needs a sunny, open site with deep, stone-free, well-drained, fertile soil that has had plenty of organic matter incorporated. To prevent plants bolting or producing stringy leaf stalks, keep them growing steadily.

Sowing

Sow seed in trays or peat pots under protection from early to late spring. Place seed on the surface of the potting mix. Self-blanching celery needs warmth to germinate – the temperature should be above 10°C (50°F).

Cultivation

About eight weeks after sowing, harden off the seedlings in a cold frame. From late spring on, when the plants have developed five to six 'true' leaves, plant them out. Celery needs plenty of water to grow quickly and remain crisp.

Harvesting

Harvesting for trench celery can begin in late autumn, when the leaf stalks are crunchy to eat; the pink and red forms are the hardiest and will be harvested last. Dig out the soil around each plant, lift the celery, then cut off the head and roots. Self-blanching celery can be harvested from mid-summer onwards. Celery can be left in the ground over winter.

H to 60cm (24in)
S to 15cm (6in)

16–18°C
(61–64°F)

Full sun

Kohlrabi

Brassica oleracea 'Gongylodes' group

Kohlrabi is grown for its nutritious, globe-like, swollen stem. There are green- and purple-skinned forms, both of which grow to 60cm (24in). Kohlrabi thrives in hot, dry conditions, and at the height of summer the stems will be ready to harvest eight weeks from sowing.

Sowing

Sow seed thinly in drills 2cm (¾in) deep and 30cm (12in) apart, in a well-prepared, finely sifted seedbed. Sow the quicker-maturing, green-skinned types from mid-spring to mid-summer, and the hardier, purple-skinned types from mid- to late summer.

Cultivation

When the first 'true' leaf develops, thin seedlings to 20cm (8in) apart.

Harvesting

The swollen stems are ready when they are 8–10cm (3–4in) across. The newer cultivars can grow much larger, because they remain tender. Cut through the taproot just below the swollen stem.

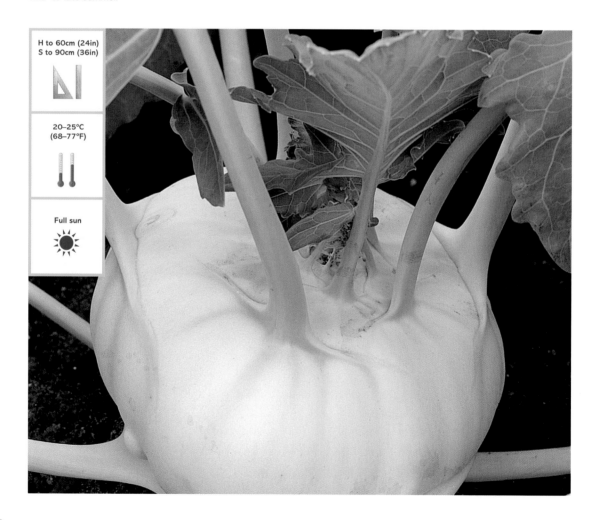

H to 60cm (24in)
S to 90cm (36in)

20–25°C
(68–77°F)

Full sun

Florence fennel

Foeniculum vulgare 'Azoricum' group

Florence fennel is grown for its succulent bulb, which has a distinctive aniseed flavour, the edible part being the swollen bases of its decorative, feathery leaves.

It prefers well-drained but moisture-retentive, fertile soil that has had plenty of organic matter incorporated six to eight weeks before planting. The bulbs are ready to harvest about 14 weeks after sowing.

Sowing

Sow seed in modules under protection from early spring onwards. Set in a temperature of 16°C (61°F) if growing in a greenhouse; seeds germinated in a polytunnel require 12–14°C (54–57°F), or 10°C (50°F) in a cold frame.

Cultivation

About six weeks after sowing, harden off the seedlings in a cold frame. Plant them out from early summer onwards, after two 'true' leaves have developed, in rows 30cm (12in) apart and with 40cm (16in) between plants. When the bulbs begin to swell, cover the lower half with soil to blanch them.

Harvesting

The bulbs will be ready to harvest from late summer onwards, when they are 10cm (4in) across. Cut them off at soil level and trim away the leaves. Fennel can withstand light frost only, and does not store well.

Rhubarb

Rheum × *hybridum*, syn. *R.* × *cultorum*

Often regarded as a fruit, but technically a vegetable, this herbaceous perennial is grown for its edible leaf stalks, which can be used for desserts and jam-making from mid-spring onwards. Rhubarb, which matures to a height of 30cm (12in), can be grown in the same plot for many years, but the well-drained, fertile soil must be dug deeply and plenty of organic matter incorporated prior to planting.

Cultivation

In late autumn, early winter or spring, plant one-year-old crowns about 1m (3ft) apart, with the young shoots ('eyes') just above soil level. If they are planted too deeply, the eyes will rot away. Mulch the crowns well, keep the soil moist, and provide generous amounts of a balanced fertiliser after harvesting. Cut off any flowering spikes as they emerge in the spring and summer, and remove any spindly, unwanted leaves as they occur.

Harvesting

Pick the rhubarb when the stalks are 30cm (12in) long and deep pink in colour. Grip each stalk as close to its base as possible and twist it gently away from the crown. Discard the leaves, because they are not edible.

H to 60cm (24in)
S to 90cm (36in)

16–18°C (61–64°F)

Full sun

H to 60cm (24in)
S to 90cm (36in)

16–18°C (61–64°F)

Partial shade

Onions
Allium cepa

The strong-flavoured bulbs of onions are invaluable in the kitchen for a wide range of dishes. They are grown as annual plants, with the brown- or yellow-skinned cultivars being the most popular with gardeners.

Onions have a long growing season, and for good skin quality and colour the bulbs need plenty of bright sunshine in the period just before harvesting. Onions prefer a well-drained, fertile soil that has been well dug.

Sowing
In early autumn or early spring, sow seed in furrows 1.25cm (½in) deep and about 30cm (12in) apart, with 2.5cm (1in) between the seeds.

Cultivation
Onions suffer from weed competition, and keeping the plants weed-free by hoeing between rows until they establish (this takes about six weeks) is critical.

Harvesting
Onions are ready for harvesting when the leaves turn yellow and the tops keel over. The process can be speeded up by bending over the tops by hand, but this must be done carefully or the bulb may be bruised and will start to rot when in store. Lift the bulbs gently with a garden fork and allow them to dry naturally before storing in a cool, dry, frost-free place.

H to 60cm (24in)
S to 20cm (8in)

16–18°C
(61–64°F)

Full sun

Spring (salad) onions

Allium cepa

Also known as bunching onions or scallions, they are fast-growing and can be used as an intercrop between larger-growing varieties or between carrots as a companion plant.

Sowing

Sow in drills every three to four weeks from early spring to late summer. Space seeds about 3cm (1¼in) apart, with 15cm (6in) between rows. There is no need to thin further.

Cultivation

Keep weed-free and water in dry conditions.

Harvesting

Ready in 8–10 weeks. As soon as they reach a reasonable size, pull alternate plants as needed.

H to 60cm (24in)
S to 20cm (8in)

16–18°C
(61–64°F)

Full sun

Garlic
Allium sativum

This hardy vegetable, with its characteristic strong flavour that makes such a valuable contribution to both cooked dishes and salads, is far easier to grow than many gardeners realise. There are two distinct forms – one white and the other purple.

Garlic has a long growing period, but will survive outdoors throughout the winter if grown in a light, dry, well-drained soil. On wetter soils, the plants should be grown on ridges to improve drainage.

Sowing
Dig over the soil deeply before planting in autumn. Split the bulbs into individual 'cloves' and push these into the soil, so that the top (pointed end) of the clove is approximately 2.5cm (1in) below the soil surface. For maximum yields and even bulb development, plant the cloves in a square arrangement at a spacing of 18cm (7in).

Cultivation
As they develop, the bulbs will gradually work their way up to the surface of the soil.

Harvesting
The bulbs will be ready to harvest as soon as the leaves begin to turn from green to yellow. Lift the bulbs gently with a garden fork and allow them to dry naturally before storing in a cool, dry, frost-free place.

H to 60cm (24in)
S to 20cm (8in)

16–18°C
(61–64°F)

Full sun

Shallots

Allium cepa 'Aggregatum' group

Shallots have a very distinctive flavour and are easy to grow, but need a longer time in the ground than onions.

Sowing

Sow seed indoors in early spring, then plant outside in late spring, 15cm (6in) apart with 23–30cm (9–12in) between rows. Plant sets in situ in late winter (traditionally the shortest day), with the tips just showing, 15cm (6in) apart with 23–30cm (9–12in) between rows.

Cultivation

It is important to keep the site weed-free. Mulch to retain moisture. Water and feed spring-sown onions until mid-summer, then water only if they start to wilt. Feed overwintered bulbs once in early spring; cover with fleece to protect from frost if bulbs start to lift from the soil.

Harvesting

Ready in 26 weeks. Lift when the leaves die down, leave to dry out, then store as for onions. Healthy bulbs can be saved for replanting the following season.

H to 60cm (24in)
S to 20cm (8in)

16–18°C
(61–64°F)

Full sun

Beetroot
Beta vulgaris

This useful root vegetable is a biennial plant that is grown as an annual, and can be used at just about any time of year either fresh, stored, or pickled. Although the round beetroot is the most common, other shapes, such as oval, flat and oblong, are grown as well. There is also a wide variation in colour – red is the most popular, but golden forms, such as 'Burpee's Golden', and white ones are available.

Sowing
Sow seeds from mid-spring through to late summer. Soak the seed in warm water for half an hour before sowing to promote rapid germination, then sow thinly in furrows 2cm (¾in) deep and 30cm (12in) apart.

Cultivation
When the seedlings are about 2.5cm (1in) high, thin them to 8–10cm (3–4in) apart for large beets, and 4–5cm (1½–2in) to produce small, round beets for pickling.

Harvesting
Harvesting usually runs from early summer to mid-autumn, although beetroot can be harvested at any stage of growth depending on the size of beetroots required. The plants are not fully hardy, however, and should all be lifted for storage by late autumn. Dig up the beetroots with a garden fork and twist off the leaves, then use immediately or store the roots in a box of moist sand in a cool, dry, frost-free place.

H to 23cm (9in)
S to 25cm (10in)

16–18°C
(61–64°F)

Partial shade

Swedes

Brassica napus 'Napobrassica' group

This cream- to purple-skinned vegetable is one of the hardiest of all root crops and is grown for its mild, sweet-tasting, yellow flesh. Good cultivars are 'York' and 'American Purple Tops'.

Swedes require similar soil conditions to turnips. The roots will be ready to harvest about 24 weeks after sowing.

Sowing

Sow seed thinly in furrows 2cm (¾in) deep and 40cm (16in) apart in a finely sifted, well-prepared seedbed, from late spring onwards.

Cultivation

The soil should not be allowed to dry out at any stage, or a large proportion of the crop will develop forked roots and the plants may bolt. When the seedlings are 2.5cm (1in) high, thin them to 8–10cm (3–4in) apart, and then thin again three weeks later to leave the plants 25cm (10in) apart.

Harvesting

Swedes are usually ready to harvest from early to mid-autumn onwards. Although they survive well outdoors through the winter, the low temperatures often give the flesh a fibrous or woody texture. It is therefore advisable to lift them and store indoors.

H to 23cm (9in)
S to 25cm (10in)

16–18°C
(61–64°F)

Partial shade

Turnips
Brassica rapa 'Rapifera' group

Often regarded as winter vegetables, turnips can be available throughout the year if a range of cultivars are grown in succession.

Turnips mature quickly and can easily be grown in a small container. They are mainly known as an ingredient of winter stews, but young turnips harvested when they are the size of golf balls are delicious.

Turnips prefer a light, fertile, well-drained but moisture-retentive soil that is high in nitrogen.

Sowing
Sow seed thinly in furrows 2cm (¾in) deep and 25–30cm (10–12in) apart in a finely sifted, well-prepared seedbed and subsequently at three-week intervals from late spring until mid- to late summer.

Cultivation
The soil should never be allowed to dry out, or much of the crop will develop forked roots and the plants may bolt. When seedlings are no higher than 2.5cm (1in), thin to 10cm (4in) apart for early cultivars, 15cm (6in) for later, hardy cultivars.

Harvesting
Turnips will be ready to harvest from early to mid-autumn, but must be lifted by mid-winter.

H to 60cm (24in)
S to 20cm (8in)

16–18°C
(61–64°F)

Partial shade

Carrots
Daucus carota

Carrots are one of the most versatile of vegetables. You can grow them in one form or another throughout the year, from the young pencil carrots that are ready in early summer to the semi-mature roots that can be lifted later in the summer and through the autumn. These are followed by the mature vegetables that are stored for use over the winter. Carrots must have a deep and fertile soil that is able to hold plenty of moisture. In particular, you need to grow the early varieties quickly if they are to be tender and tasty. Never grow carrots on land that has just had compost or manure dug in, as they usually produce divided roots. For the earliest crops of tender, young carrots, broadcast the seed, rather than sow it in rows, during early spring.

Cultivation
Thin the seedlings to 4–7cm (1½–2¾in) apart for medium-sized carrots and 7–10cm (2¾–4in) for larger carrots suitable for storing through the winter. Thinning is best done in the evening or in cool, dull conditions to deter carrot rust fly. Hoe between the rows until foliage shades the soil and reduces weeds.

Harvesting
Early carrots can be eased out with a fork and then pulled by hand. Dig up maincrop carrots with a fork for immediate use, freezing or storing. Twist off and then discard the foliage.

H to 30cm (12in)
S to 8cm (3in)

16–18°C
(61–64°F)

Full sun

Jerusalem artichokes

Helianthus tuberosus

Grown for its edible root, the hardy Jerusalem artichoke is also used to help to clear rough ground. A vigorous perennial and relative of the sunflower, it can grow to a height of 3m (10ft), although the cultivar 'Dwarf Sunray' will reach only about 1.8m (6ft).

Cultivation

Plant purchased tubers in spring, 10–15cm (4–6in) deep, in deeply cultivated soil. Plant in rows 60cm (24in) apart, with 30cm (12in) between the tubers. Large tubers can be divided up so that each piece has a separate shoot, and the sections planted individually. When the plants are 30cm (12in) high, mound up the soil 15cm (6in) high around the base to keep the plants stable. In summer, cut the stems down to 1.5m (5ft) to encourage tuber formation. In dry weather, irrigate to keep the tubers swelling.

Harvesting

The tubers are ready from mid-autumn onwards and should be dug up with a garden fork. In well-drained soils the tubers can be overwintered in the growing site. When harvesting, remove all parts of the tubers from the soil, or they will resprout next season.

H to 3m (10ft)
S to 30cm (12in)

16–18°C
(61–64°F)

Full sun

Parsnips
Pastinaca sativa

These winter vegetables have a very distinctive flavour and are hardy enough to overwinter in the soil. Parsnips prefer a deep, stone-free, well-drained, fertile soil, but on shallow soils shorter-rooted cultivars can be used.

Sowing
Sow seed thinly in furrows 1.25cm (½in) deep and 30cm (12in) apart, in early spring. Fresh seed gives the best results.

Cultivation
When the seedlings are about 2.5cm (1in) high, thin them to 7–10cm (2¾–4in) apart to produce large roots suitable for overwintering.

Harvesting
The roots will be ready to be lifted from mid-autumn onwards. Dig them up with a fork.

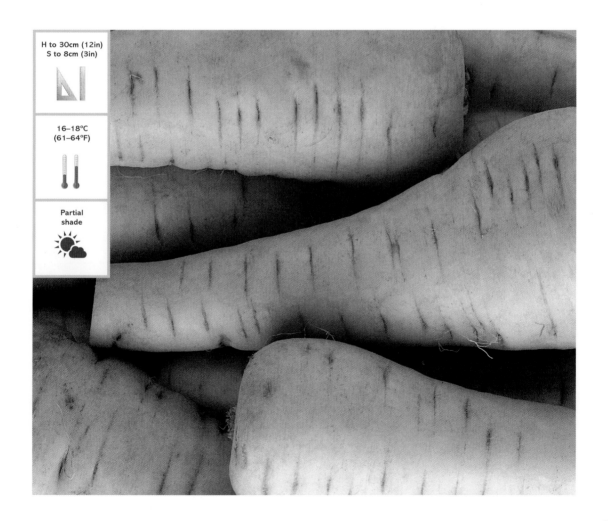

H to 30cm (12in)
S to 8cm (3in)

16–18°C
(61–64°F)

Partial shade

Radish

Raphanus sativus

One of the easiest of all vegetables to grow, radishes are the best way to introduce children to gardening. They germinate easily and mature quickly, in about a month. Gardeners with large vegetable gardens often use them as a marker crop between rows of vegetables that take longer to germinate, and for the adventurous there are a number of winter-maturing radishes and the giant Japanese mooli radishes.

Sowing

Sow seed thinly in furrows 1.25cm (½in) deep and about 15cm (6in) apart. For a continuous supply, sow seed at 10-day intervals from early spring through to early autumn. The seed will keep for up to 10 years if kept cool and stored in an airtight container.

Cultivation

Radishes produce poor plants if overcrowded, and ideally they should be about 2.5cm (1in) apart. Watering is essential: drought will make the roots woody or encourage the plants to bolt.

Harvesting

Radishes are ready to harvest when the roots are about 2.5cm (1in) across at their widest point. Grip the plant firmly by its leaves and pull gently. If the soil is dry, water the plants the day before harvesting so that they will pull out of the ground easily.

H to 30cm (12in)
S to 8cm (3in)

16–18°C
(61–64°F)

Partial
shade

Black salsify

Scorzonera hispanica

This hardy, perennial plant is, like carrots, usually grown as an annual for its thick, fleshy roots. These are about 20cm (8in) long and have a shiny, black skin – and a distinctive flavour when cooked. The young shoots (chards) and flower buds are also edible. It needs to have a deep, fertile soil in order to do well and produce a good crop.

Sowing
Sow seed thinly in furrows 1.25cm (½in) deep and 20cm (8in) apart, in spring.

Cultivation
Thin the seedlings to 10cm (4in) apart soon after germination. In order to achieve maximum growth, keep the plants weed-free and make sure they are well watered.

Harvesting
The roots will be ready to harvest from late autumn onwards. In mild areas the roots can be lifted and used immediately, but in colder areas they should be lifted and stored in boxes of sand before winter weather sets in.

Roots that are overwintered in the ground can be covered with straw in early spring. Young shoots will emerge through the straw, and these (and the flower buds) can be harvested when they are about 10cm (4in) high.

H to 60cm (24in)
S to 30cm (12in)

16–18°C
(61–64°F)

Full sun

Potato

Solanum tuberosum

This versatile vegetable is divided into three main groups: earlies (quicker-growing cultivars); maincrop (slower-growing cultivars, producing heavier crops); and mid-season, which mature between the other two. Most early-season potatoes are ready to harvest from early summer onwards, and do not store well. Maincrop potatoes are available from mid-summer through into winter and can be stored.

Sowing
'Seed' is the term used for young potato tubers that are planted to produce the next crop. Purchase good-quality 'seed' potatoes in late winter and arrange the tubers in shallow trays to chit (sprout) in early spring.

Cultivation
In most areas planting can commence from mid-spring onwards for earlies, finishing with the last of the maincrop tubers by early to mid-summer. Plant the tubers 40cm (16in) apart, in rows 60cm (24in) apart.

Harvesting
Early potatoes are ready for lifting when the flowers start to open. To harvest, use a garden fork to dig under the ridge of earth and ease the tubers from the soil to avoid 'stabbing' them.

H to 45cm (18in)
S to 60cm (24in)

16–18°C
(61–64°F)

Partial
shade

Salsify
Tragopogon porrifolius

A hardy biennial plant, salsify is usually grown for its cream-white, fleshy roots, although its shoots are also edible. Because of its delicious flavour, it is often called the 'vegetable oyster'.

In order to achieve maximum growth, salsify requires a deep, well-drained, fertile soil.

Sowing
Sow seed in furrows 1.25cm (½in) deep and 15cm (6in) apart, in spring. Fresh seed gives the best results, since salsify seed loses viability very quickly.

Cultivation
Thin the seedlings to 10cm (4in) apart soon after germination. To encourage rapid growth, keep the plants weed-free and well watered.

Harvesting
The roots will be ready to harvest from late autumn onwards. In mild areas the roots can be lifted and used as required, but in colder areas the roots should be lifted and stored in boxes of sand before winter frost sets in.

H to 60cm (24in)
S to 30cm (12in)

16–18°C
(61–64°F)

Full sun

Herbs

Lemon verbena

Aloysia triphylla

Lemon verbena forms a woody shrub in its natural habitat, and is cultivated chiefly for the amazing lemon scent of its leaves.

In mild climates it can be grown outdoors in sheltered positions, on light, well-drained soil. As it is only half-hardy, it is normally best grown in a container. In winter, before any hard frosts, move the container indoors. The plant will be dormant over the winter and come into leaf in late spring. Cut it back to shape at this stage, and you will have a decorative and highly scented shrub to put out on the patio. Lemon verbena is prone to infestation by red spider mites. Use cold-water sprays or insecticidal soap to control them.

The leaves of lemon verbena make a delicious tea, which is soothing for digestion, and add a delightful lemon fragrance to many dishes. Always harvest the leaves before the plant flowers.

Care

Lemon verbena prefers rich, well-drained soil and a site in full sun.

New plants

Take semi-ripe cuttings in summer, and keep under plastic or mist. The seeds of this plant are rarely obtainable.

H to 1.8m (6ft)
S to 1.2m (4ft)

18–20°C
(64–68°F)

Full sun

Chamomile

Anthemis

With their small, white, daisy-like flowers, all the chamomiles make attractive garden plants and form a decorative, creeping ground cover. The wonderful apple-scented foliage provides fragrant lawns. With a maximum height of 15cm (6in), the double cream form illustrated is a lovely low-growing plant for the rock garden, the front of a border, or a formal herb garden. *Anthemis nobile* grows to 30cm (12in) high in flower and looks equally good in the border or herb garden. As a lawn herb it needs to be cut regularly, although the non-flowering clone, 'Treneague', requires no cutting. *A. tinctoria*, with larger, yellow flowers, is known as dyer's chamomile and produces bright yellow dyes. It grows 60cm (24in) high, and the foliage is not apple-scented.

Chamomile, one of the oldest garden herbs, was revered by the ancient Egyptians for its curative powers. For centuries it has been grown in herb gardens both for decoration and for its medicinal properties.

Care

Chamomile prefers well-drained, sandy soil and a site in full sun, although it will tolerate partial shade.

New plants

Sow seeds in spring in fine soil; divide plants in spring.

H to 60cm (24in)
S to 30cm (12in)

16–18°C
(61–64°F)

Full sun or
partial shade

189

Artemisia
Artemisia

The genus *Artemisia* contains a wide range of silver-grey foliage plants and several aromatic herbs, including *Artemisia absinthium* (wormwood), *A. abrotanum* (southernwood), *A. pontica* (Roman wormwood), and the indispensable culinary herb *A. dracunculus* (French tarragon). All these herbs, except the last, have particularly decorative leaves and, with their silver-grey colouring, are invaluable in mixed plantings.

Wormwood, or green ginger as it is also known, is an outstanding foliage herb, especially the variety 'Lambrook Silver', and is undemanding in its requirements.

Wormwood is a bitter herb and was used to make the potent drink absinthe. The attractive green-grey foliage of southernwood has a fragrant fruity scent. Roman wormwood has finely divided and fragrant leaves. *A. ludoviciana* (western mugwort) is an exceptionally decorative plant.

Care
All varieties seem to thrive in drought conditions, but they do demand good winter drainage as they will not survive with waterlogged soil around their roots. The ground-cover varieties require a covering of grit or gravel, to keep wet soil off their foliage.

New plants
Sow seeds in late summer; take semi-ripe cuttings in summer; divide in autumn.

H to 1.5m (5ft)
S 90cm to (36in)

15–17°C (59–62°F)

Full sun

Garden calamint
Calamintha grandiflora

Garden calamint, also known as mountain balm, is a small, bushy plant with mint-scented leaves. The small, pink, sage-like flowers continue for a long season.

Grow calamint near the edge of the border, where its scent can be appreciated and its attractive flowers enjoyed. It looks good in the rock garden, but needs to be out of the hottest sun in light or partial shade, and can also be grown in the dappled shade of trees or on a hedge bank.

Garden calamint has some healing properties, although it cannot be considered an important medicinal plant. A tisane made from either fresh or dried leaves is refreshing and a mild tonic. John Gerard, the English herbalist, recommended calamint for the cure of melancholy, so this is a tea that could be a pleasant pick-me-up during the dull days of winter.

Care
Garden calamint will tolerate most soils if they are well drained. It requires a site in partial shade.

New plants
Sow seeds in spring; divide in autumn or spring; take cuttings in spring.

H to 60cm (24in)
S to 45cm (18in)

15–17°C (59–62°F)

Partial shade

Burning bush

Dictamnus purpureus

Burning bush is so called because the flowers give off an inflammable vapour in hot, dry conditions. The whole plant is also highly aromatic, reminiscent of lemon peel and balsam.

Burning bush is also sometimes known as white (or purple) dittany or fraxinella. It is not related to and should not be confused with the other dittany, *Origanum dictamnus* (dittany of Crete), which is a member of the mint family.

Burning bush is a magnificent-looking plant that should have a lightly shaded position in a border, with a fairly dry loam soil. Grow it with other plants that enjoy similar conditions, such as *Filipendula vulgaris* (dropwort), *Linum perenne* (perennial flax) and *Pulsatilla vulgaris* (pasqueflower).

The plant has been used medicinally in the past but is little valued today. The scented leaves provide a tea substitute.

Care

Burning bush likes well-drained alkaline loam and a site in partial shade.

New plants

Sow seeds fresh in late summer; divide in spring; take root cuttings in late autumn or early winter.

H to 90cm (36in)
S to 45cm (18in)

15–17°C
(59–62°F)

Partial shade

Curry plant
Helichrysum angustifolium

The curry plant is a fairly recent introduction to the herb garden and something of a novelty. Brushing against this plant is an extraordinary experience as the aroma of curry is mysteriously released. This shrub retains its silver-grey foliage through the winter months, and is very drought-resistant. The dwarf variety 'Nanum' is superb for the rock garden and makes a neat edging for a formal herb or knot garden.

The one vital growth requirement for curry plant is sharp drainage. It is pretty hardy, but will not survive wet, cold soil over winter. Clip it lightly after flowering and again in spring.

Although curry plant is not really a culinary herb, it can be used experimentally to give the subtlest curry flavour to soups, stews and vegetables.

Care
Curry plant prefers sharply drained and not too fertile soil. It requires a site in full sun.

New plants
Take soft or semi-ripe cuttings in spring and summer.

H to 60cm (24in)
S to 60cm (24in)

15–17°C
(59–62°F)

Full sun

Heliotrope

Heliotropium arborescens

Heliotrope is so named because its flowers move with the sun. This is a beautifully scented plant, which bears dense clusters of vivid purple, sweetly fragrant flowers over a long period. The semi-glossy foliage is an attractive burnished purple.

In warm, frost-free climates heliotrope grows into a small, bushy shrub. In areas with cold winters it should be treated as an annual and either planted out after the danger of frost is over or grown in a container. It thrives in most good soils, but needs some moisture. Position it near the house, where its scent can be appreciated.

Heliotrope flowers are excellent in potpourri, and the herb was once used in homeopathic medicine.

Care
This plant prefers fertile, well-drained soil and a site in full sun.

New plants
Sow seeds in spring; take cuttings in summer. Germination of the seeds occurs at about 21°C (70°F) and takes approximately three weeks. Softwood cuttings can easily be taken, and this is often worth doing to maintain a plant with a particularly strong scent.

H to 60cm (24in)
S to 60cm (24in)

18–20°C
(64–68°F)

Full sun

Sweet rocket

Hesperis matronalis

Sweet rocket is also called dame's violet and vesper flower because the flowers emit their scent only after sunset. Do not confuse it with *Eruca sativa* (the annual Mediterranean rocket, or arugula), a salad herb.

Sweet rocket is vigorous and can grow tall in the right conditions, so give it space. Plant it near the house so that its evening scent can be fully appreciated. The plant should be allowed to self-seed in a planting in sun or light shade. The lovely white form should always be grown in some shade; against a dark background it looks cool and striking.

The leaves of sweet rocket are used to add a bitter tang to green salads. Collect them before the plant flowers.

Medicinally, this herb is used as an antiscorbutic because it has a high vitamin C content.

Care
Sweet rocket prefers rich, moisture-retaining loam, but is tolerant of poor soil. It requires a site in full sun, but it will tolerate partial shade.

New plants
Sow seeds in spring or late summer; take basal cuttings in spring.

H to 1.5m (5ft)
S to 60cm (24in)

15–17°C
(59–62°F)

Full sun or
partial shade

Lavender
Lavandula

Lavender, which must be among the most well known of all scented herbs, keeps its grey-green leaves over winter and flowers for many weeks. A huge number of species and varieties are available.

Lavenders in great variety are ideal for edging and hedging. They can be kept neatly clipped after the flowers are over. If plants become too large, cutting back more severely in spring will improve them. For a tall hedge 'Old English' or 'Grappenhall' are the largest-growing plants. There are several good, intermediate-sized lavenders and a wide choice of dwarf lavenders from which to select your preferred flower and foliage colour.

Medicinally, lavender is used as a mild sedative, an antiseptic, an antispasmodic and a carminative. The essential oil derived from lavender is one of the most valuable and has many applications.

Care
Grow in well-drained, alkaline soil that is not too rich. This plant needs full sun in order to thrive.

New plants
Sow seeds in autumn; take greenwood cuttings in spring and hardwood cuttings in summer or autumn.

h to 90cm (36in)
S to 90cm (36in)

18–20°C
(64–68°F)

Full sun

Lemon balm
Melissa officinalis

An easy and undemanding herb to grow, lemon balm will withstand considerable heat and drought, and will even flourish at the base of a sunny wall. It is not a particularly decorative plant, but if cut down after flowering it will remain neat and green, and will also produce more leaf for cutting. However, *Melissa officinalis* 'Aurea' (golden lemon balm) is worth growing for its pretty gold-and-green, variegated leaves, and the variety *M. officinalis* 'All Gold' is also highly recommended. These golden balms look and do best in a little shade; otherwise the leaves tend to brown.

The Arabs regard lemon balm as a valuable medicinal plant, with particular benefit for treating anxiety and depression, and as a sedative and tonic tea. The ancient Greeks grew it as an important bee plant and for its scented foliage.

Care
Lemon balm enjoys fairly fertile, well-drained loam and a site in partial shade.

New plants
Divide roots or sow seeds in spring (germination can be erratic); take cuttings in spring and early summer.

H to 60cm (24in)
S to 45cm (18in)

18–20°C
(64–68°F)

Partial
shade

Mint
Mentha

Mints worth growing are: *Mentha spicata* 'Moroccan', the best for mint sauce and mint drinks; *M.* x *piperita piperita* (peppermint), also available with decorative crisped leaves; *M.* x *piperita* var. *citrata* (bergamot or eau de Cologne mint), with red-tinged, scented foliage; *M. suaveolens* (apple mint), and also its white-variegated form, *M. s.* 'Variegata', often known as pineapple mint; and the vigorous, woolly leaved *M.* x *villosa alopecuroides* 'Bowles' (Bowles mint), which gives a superb flavour to mint sauce and new potatoes.

Mints require a rich, well-drained loam that will retain moisture in summer. If they are put under stress with too few nutrients or, more important, too little moisture, they become unhealthy and susceptible to rust and – in the case of woolly leaved mints – to mildew.

Mints, especially peppermint and spearmint, are valuable medicinally and make a delightful and soothing tea. Eau de Cologne or bergamot mint is used in perfumes and soaps.

Care
Mints like fertile, well-drained, moist loam and a site in full sun, although they will tolerate partial shade.

New plants
Divide runners in autumn; root cuttings in water or compost in spring and early summer.

H to 60cm (24in)
S indefinite

16–18°C
(61–64°F)

Full sun or
partial shade

Rose
Rosa

The rose is our most popular and best-loved garden plant. There are said to be over 10,000 cultivated varieties.

The rose is an extremely versatile plant: there is one for every garden. Most prefer a rich, fertile loam soil that is clay-based and retains moisture. However, there are varieties that will grow in sandy or poor conditions, and many that will tolerate some shade. Many roses make excellent decorative hedges, but most are used in the garden as specimen shrubs, climbers or ramblers. A mixed selection can also be planted into a specially prepared bed.

Today attar of roses is one of the most popular ingredients of perfume, soaps and cosmetics. Although the rose is now little used medicinally, the essential oil is valued in aromatherapy to treat many conditions. Rose hips are extensively used as a rich source of vitamin C. Rose petals are indispensable in potpourri; they retain their fragrance for a long period and also keep their colour well when dried.

Care
Roses are tolerant of soil type but do best in clay-based loam. They prefer a site in full sun or partial shade.

New plants
Sow seeds of species in autumn (stratify); try layering in mid-summer; take cuttings of current year's growth in early autumn.

H to 1.2m (4ft)
S to 90cm (36in)

18–20°C
(64–68°F)

Full sun or
partial shade

Santolina

Santolina

Santolina, or cotton lavender, looks nothing like lavender and is in no way related to it. However, its finely cut foliage is just as decorative and as useful in the herb garden.

Santolina grows naturally on dry, stony soils that are baked by the hot Mediterranean sun, so this is a plant that will survive heat and dry soil conditions.

There is a good variety of santolinas available for the garden, each with its own distinctive texture, such as *Santolina chamaecyparissus* 'Lemon Queen'. This has lovely, soft lemon-coloured flowers and a low-spreading habit, which provides excellent ground cover in dry, stony areas; it is a decorative rock garden plant. Santolina makes a superb hedge, especially the compact form: it can be kept tightly clipped and shaped, and looks good all year round.

The shrub was used medicinally but nowadays is more valued for decorative use, in both fresh and dried forms, and as an insect repellent.

Care
Santolina prefers well-drained, alkaline soil, dry in summer. It requires a site in full sun.

New plants
Take tip cuttings in spring or summer.

H to 60cm
(24in)
S to 45cm
(18in)

15–17°C
(59–62°F)

Full sun

Sweet violet

Viola odorata

This lovely herb has always been the harbinger of spring. Every garden, however small it is, should have sweet violets growing in some shady corner, perhaps around a tree, among shrubs, or at the edge of woodland where there is shade during the hottest part of the day. Violets will also establish themselves in short grass. They need some moisture and enjoy a woodland-type soil with plenty of leaf mould. A few plants will soon spread in suitable conditions. Sweet violets look best growing with other wild woodland herbs, such as primroses, oxlips, hellebores, wild strawberries and lungwort. Grow violets in earthenware containers, which can be brought into the house in winter and placed on a windowsill.

Medicinally, sweet violet is valued for its soothing expectorant properties in the treatment of respiratory disorders, including bronchitis. It alleviates and cools hot swellings, and is also mildly sedative. The flowers are extensively used in perfumery and can be candied. In Britain the flowers were cooked with meat and game.

Care
Violets like moisture-retaining to moist, humus-rich, alkaline soil and a site in partial shade.

New plants
Sow seeds in autumn; divide in late winter or early spring.

H to 15cm
(6in),
S indefinite

15–17°C
(59–62°F)

Partial
shade

Chives

Allium schoenoprasum

Chives have particularly pretty, pink to purple flower heads and make a lovely edging for a border or formal herb garden. Even when not in flower, the clumps of lush green, cylindrical, hollow stems are attractive.

Chives prefer a fertile soil with some moisture, but will grow in surprisingly dry conditions, including gravel or the rock garden. To propagate, divide into clumps of half a dozen small bulbs and replant during the spring. Chives die down completely in winter.

Chives have become a popular and indispensable seasoning, imparting a delicate onion flavour. The flowers can be used to decorate and flavour salads and soups.

Care
Chives prefer moist, rich loam in direct sunlight.

New plants
Sow in seed trays indoors in spring and then plant out in groups of three or four seedlings. Established groups can be divided every three or four years in spring or autumn.

Garlic

Allium sativum

Common garlic can be classed either as a herb or a vegetable. It is a close relation of the onion, and its growth habit and appearance are similar. Garlic is probably the most commonly used herb in the kitchen. Many famous dishes are based on garlic, such as *aïoli*, a garlicky mayonnaise dip from Provence.

Garlic is also much valued in herbal medicine, as a digestive and in the treatment of high blood pressure. It is also supposed to ward off the common cold.

Care
Garlic prefers fertile, sandy to moist loam and a site in full sun, although it will tolerate partial shade.

New plants
Plant individual cloves in the autumn approximately 10cm (4in) deep and 18cm (7in) apart; most varieties need at least two months at temperatures between 0°C (32°F) and 10°C (50°F). Do not plant on ground that has been recently manured.

H to 30cm (12in)
S to 30cm (12in)

15–17°C (60–62°F)

Full sun

H to 30cm (12in)
S to 30cm (12in)

15–17°C (59–62°F)

Full sun or partial shade

Dill
Anethum graveolens

All forms of dill are decorative at every stage of growth. With its feathery foliage, dill looks pretty in a border or in a formal herb garden and produces attractive flower and seed heads, which dry well.

Dill should be grown in a clump or mass. Sow it in spring by broadcasting the seeds. In order to obtain a good leaf harvest, use the most suitable variety and make sure that the plants do not dry out, as they will go straight up to flower.

Dill has always been an essential flavouring in Scandinavian cooking, where it is used in pickling and fish dishes, most famously in gravadlax, salmon pickled with dill. The seeds are used extensively for pickling cucumbers and to flavour bread and cakes. The chopped leaves are sprinkled on many dishes. Dill seed is good for the digestion.

Care
Dill tolerates most soils and resists drought. It prefers a site in full sun.

New plants
Sow seeds in spring, or plant in succession for culinary use.

H to 90cm (36in)
S to 30cm (12in)

16–18°C
(61–64°F)

Full sun

Angelica

Angelica archangelica

The stately angelica is a striking plant by any standards. It should be grown for its decorative and architectural value as a specimen. Plant either near water or in a mixed border. In the first year angelica normally produces only a large leafy rosette. It will self-seed profusely.

Angelica stem is used as a green candied cake decoration. The herb is also an ingredient of certain liqueurs, such as Benedictine. Medicinally, it is used as an infusion to treat bronchitis, flatulence and colds.

Care

Angelica likes soil that is rich, deep and moist, either in full sunlight or light shade.

New plants

Sow fresh seeds where you wish the plants to grow, in the autumn. Transplant these to 90cm (36in) apart during the spring.

Warning Angelica can be mistaken in the wild for water hemlock, which is very poisonous and favours a similar habitat.

H to 2.1m (7ft)
S to 90cm (36in)

18–20°C
(64–68°F)

Full sun

Chervil

Anthriscus cerefolium

An attractive herb with extremely delicate, fern-like leaves and pretty white flowers, chervil is very short-lived in many situations and goes rapidly to seed. However, the seedlings make a fine ground cover.

Chervil does best in cool, slightly moist conditions. Grow it where it will receive sun in winter but will be shaded as the sun heats up. It is best sown in late summer for a winter and spring crop, and again in early spring to produce leaf in early summer.

As a culinary herb chervil should be more widely used. In France it is appreciated as an ingredient of *fines herbes* and *bouquet garni*. The flavour is very delicate, with a hint of aniseed. It is used to flavour soups and stews, and should be added at the last minute otherwise the flavour will be lost in cooking.

Care
Chervil prefers light soil with humus and some moisture. It requires a site that is partially shady in summer.

New plants
Sow seeds in spring and late summer where the plants are to grow. Thin plants to 15cm (6in) apart and water regularly during the summer. Seeds sown in early spring will mature in the summer. Seeds sown in late summer will produce leaves over the winter.

H to 60cm (24in)
S to 30cm (12in)

18–20°C
(64–68°F)

Partial shade

Horseradish
Armoracia rusticana

Horseradish is a perennial plant of the *Brassicaceae* family, which also includes mustard, wasabi, broccoli and cabbages. The plant is probably native to southeastern Europe and western Asia, but is popular around the world today. It grows up to 1.5m (5ft) tall and is mainly cultivated for its large, white, tapered root.

The intact horseradish root has hardly any aroma. When cut or grated, however, enzymes from the damaged plant cells break down and produce mustard oil, which irritates the sinuses and eyes. Once grated, if not used immediately or mixed in vinegar, the root darkens and loses its pungency, becoming unpleasantly bitter when exposed to air and heat.

Horseradish has been cultivated since antiquity. Both root and leaves were used as a medicine during the Middle Ages and the root was used as a condiment on meats in Germany, Scandinavia and Britain.

Care
Horseradish likes a moist, neutral soil in direct sunlight, although it will tolerate partial shade.

New plants
Propagate by dividing rhizomes, tubers, corms or bulbs (including offsets).

French tarragon
Artemisia dracunculus

This herbaceous perennial is much used in the kitchen, particularly to flavour vinegar, and was historically used to cure toothache. The leaves are also used in salads and as a seasoning. Grown as a kitchen herb, the leaves can be cut and used when young. Alternatively, cut off the flower heads as they form, and then cut and dry the stems for use during the autumn and winter. Strip the leaves from the plant when drying is complete and store them in airtight bottles. French tarragon is not totally hardy and protection may be needed in hard winters in cold districts.

Care
French tarragon prefers fertile soil mixed with crushed rocks, sand and gravel for good drainage. It requires a site in full sun and the base of the plant must not be shaded.

New plants
Sow seeds in late summer; take semi-ripe cuttings in summer; divide in the autumn.

Warning Other types of Artemisia are potentially toxic; use only *A. dracunculus* or *A. d. dracunculoides* (Russian tarragon).

H to 1.5m (5ft)
S to 60cm (24in)

15–17°C (60–62°F)

Full sun

H to 1.5m (5ft)
S to 90cm (36in)

16–18°C (61–64°F)

Full sun

Borage
Borago officinalis

Borage, or burrage, has long been grown in herb gardens and is a firm favourite because of its beautiful intense blue, star-like flowers.

Borage self-seeds readily and in good soil forms a substantial plant. If you keep bees, it is worth seeding a large patch since it will flower for months and bees love it. Borage will grow well in a container of rich soil, but will need frequent watering in hot weather.

Borage leaves impart a fresh cucumber flavour to summer drinks and should be used in fruit cups and wine cups. The young leaves make a delicious addition to a green salad, and the flowers look spectacular sprinkled over the top. The flowers can also be candied. Wonderful honey is produced from the flowers. Traditionally, borage was used to drive away sorrow and melancholy. It has well-tried medicinal properties and an infusion makes a soothing treatment for bronchitis and catarrh.

Care
Borage can be planted in most well-drained soils and thrives in full sun, although it will tolerate partial shade.

New plants
Sow the seeds in spring; divide in the autumn or spring; take cuttings in the spring.

H to 45cm (18in)
S to 45cm (18in)

18–20°C
(65–70°F)

Full sun

Caraway
Carum carvi

Caraway is closely related to dill, fennel, anise and cumin. The dainty white flower heads are set off well by its finely cut, fern-like foliage, which creates a wonderfully soft texture when grown in a clump. Sown in summer, the small plants will establish before the winter and make an attractive ground cover. They will mature the following summer. Gather seeds when they are brown and ripe.

Caraway, mentioned in the Bible and grown by the ancient Egyptians, has been in use for 5,000 years. The young leaves can be added to salads, and the root cooked as a vegetable. The seeds are extensively utilised to flavour cakes and breads, and to season vegetables, cheese and sausages. The seeds have also long been utilised medicinally, in particular to soothe digestive upsets.

Care
Caraway will grow happily in most soils, especially light ones. It prefers a site in full sun.

New plants
Sow seeds in late summer in situ. Thin to 15cm (6in) apart. The plant will carry flower heads and seeds in its second year.

H to 75cm (30in)
S to 30cm (12in)

18–20°C
(64–68°F)

Full sun

Coriander

Coriandrum sativum

Coriander is an ancient herb and spice used for over 3,000 years. An extremely beautiful plant when in flower and seed, it has decorative, glossy, bright green leaves and pretty white flowers with a pink-mauve tinge. In the herb garden coriander looks delightful, and it can also be grown in gravel, provided that there is some moisture.

Sow the large seeds from spring to summer about 1.25cm (½in) deep. For maximum leaf harvest, choose a variety specifically for leaf production and make sure that the soil is fertile and well drained; for good supplies of leaf, sow the seeds in succession.

Both coriander seeds and the fresh leaf are used extensively to flavour cakes, curries, Frankfurters, various liqueurs, pastries, bread and sweets. The seeds help to aid digestion.

Care
Coriander will grow successfully in any fertile, well-drained soil. It prefers a site in full sun.

New plants
Sow seeds in spring and early summer, and thin to 15cm (6in) apart.

H to 60cm (24in)
S to 23cm (9in)

16–18°C
(61–64°F)

Full sun

Bronze fennel

Foeniculum vulgare 'Purpureum'

Fennel provides feathery spring foliage and looks superb in almost any garden setting. The bronze variety is particularly handsome. The attractive yellow flower heads are visited by bees and other insects. Its main requirement is a hot, sunny situation and very well-drained soil.

The whole plant has an aniseed flavour, and is indispensable in many dishes, especially fish. The seeds are used to sprinkle on sweets, cakes and breads. The thick bulbous stem of the sweet, or Florence, fennel (*Foeniculum v.* var. *azoricum*) is eaten as a vegetable. Both the seeds and root of fennel are valued medicinally for their digestive properties. The tops yield bronze-green and brown dyes.

Care
This plant requires well-drained, deep soil and prefers a site in full sun.

New plants
Sow seeds in autumn or spring.

Hyssop

Hyssopus

Hyssop is an ancient herb mentioned in the Bible. It forms a woody, neat, upright shrub. When in bloom, the intense blue flowers are a glorious sight. Hyssop can be planted as a hedge or decorative border; keep it well trimmed. It looks particularly good with the lax-growing, grey-leaved catmint. If using different colours of hyssop, grow a predominance of one shade with a small proportion of other colours interspersed. Hyssop also makes an attractive specimen plant in the herb garden, and is an excellent bee and butterfly plant. *Hyssopus aristatus*, the smaller-growing mountain hyssop, which has deep blue flowers in late summer (after *H. officinalis*), is a good rock plant; its leaves are a brighter green.

Hyssop is traditionally used in liqueurs such as Benedictine and Chartreuse. In times gone by it was employed as a stewing herb, because of its strong scent and curative virtues. Medicinally, hyssop is valuable taken as an infusion to treat colds, bronchitis, sore throats and catarrh.

Care
Hyssop thrives in well-drained and rather light soil, and prefers a site that is in full sun.

New plants
Sow hyssop seeds in the spring or late summer and take cuttings in late spring or early summer.

H to 1.8m (6ft)
S to 45cm (18in)

18–20°C (64–68°F)

Full sun

H to 75cm (30in)
S to 90cm (36in)

15–17°C (59–62°F)

Full sun

Sweet bay

Laurus nobilis

The sweet bay, or sweet laurel, is one of the best-known aromatic, evergreen trees. Now grown mainly for its culinary virtues, it was once a sacred tree to the Greeks and Romans; the leaves were traditionally used to crown returning victors from the wars in Ancient Rome.

Bay should be grown in a sheltered spot protected from icy winds, which will burn its leaves and even cut it to the ground in harsh weather. It enjoys the partial shade of other trees. In areas of deep winter cold, grow bay in a container, and bring it inside during hard weather. It can be clipped to various shapes and cut back hard in late summer. Bay trees have smooth, pointed leaves that are dried and used to flavour stews.

Care
Bay will tolerate most well-drained, moisture-retaining, fertile soils. It prefers a sheltered site in full sun, although it will tolerate partial shade.

New plants
Bay is not an easy herb to propagate; buying a small plant is the best way to get started. Alternatively, sow fresh, moist seeds in autumn; take semi-ripe cuttings in late summer, best using mist and bottom heat.

H to 12m (39ft)
S to 10m (33ft)

18–20°C
(64–68°F)

Full sun

Lovage
Levisticum officinale

A large and leafy herb, lovage was a popular medicinal in the Middle Ages, when it was grown by the Benedictine monks. The ancient Greeks also valued it and chewed the small, aromatic leaves to help to relieve indigestion. The distinctive scent is close to that of celery.

In a rich soil lovage can grow to massive proportions after a few years. One plant only is required in the garden; give it ample space in full sun. When the flowers are over, cut the stems down to stop the plant falling over and self-seeding.

Lovage, formerly believed to be an aphrodisiac, was used in love potions. In the kitchen it is invaluable if used sparingly, giving a celery flavour to many dishes. The chopped leaves and young stems can be added to salads, and the seeds and leaves make a tea that is helpful in the treatment of indigestion and flatulence.

Care
Lovage prefers a rich, deep, moisture-retaining but well-drained soil. It requires a site in full sun.

New plants
Sow seeds in autumn (when ripe) or spring; divide plants in early spring.

H to 2.5m (8ft)
S to 1m (3ft)

15–17°C
(59–62°F)

Full sun

Pennyroyal

Mentha pulegium

Pennyroyal is a plant in the mint genus, within the family *Lamiaceae*. Crushed pennyroyal leaves exhibit a very strong fragrance similar to spearmint. Pennyroyal is a traditional culinary herb and folk remedy. The essential oil of pennyroyal is used in aromatherapy. It is also high in pulegone, a highly toxic, volatile organic compound affecting liver and uterine function.

Pennyroyal was commonly used as a cooking herb by the Greeks and Romans. The ancient Greeks often flavoured their wine with pennyroyal. A large number of the recipes in the Roman cookbook of Apicius call for the use of pennyroyal, often along with such herbs as lovage, oregano and coriander. Although still commonly used for cooking in the Middle Ages, it gradually fell out of use as a culinary herb and is seldom used so today.

Care
Mint likes fertile, moisture-retentive soil and a site in full sun, although it will tolerate partial shade.

New plants
By division in autumn or spring.

Spearmint

Mentha spicata

This is the most commonly grown garden mint, considered by many as the best for making mint sauce and for flavouring mint drinks in summer. Other favoured perennial mints in the kitchen are *Mentha suaveolens*, (apple mint) or its variety *M. s.* 'Variegata' , which has attractive white and green leaves, and *M.* x *villosa alopecuroides* 'Bowles', a popular mint particularly used for flavouring new potatoes. Mints, especially peppermint and spearmint, are valuable medicinals and make a delightful and soothing tea. Eau de Cologne or bergamot mint is used in perfumes and soaps. In the home mints have many applications: for instance, both peppermint and spearmint make refreshing additives to the bath.

Care
Mint likes fertile, moisture-retentive soil and a site in full sun, although it will tolerate partial shade.

New plants
By division in autumn or spring.

H to 60 cm (24in)
S to 20cm (8in)

15–17°C (60–62°F)

Full sun or partial shade

H to 60cm (24in)
S to 20cm (8in)

15–17°C (59–62°F)

Full sun or partial shade

211

Sweet cicely

Myrrhis odorata

Sweet cicely, with its soft green, fern-like leaves and white flower heads, is a lovely herb for the wild or woodland-edge garden. It has an aniseed scent. The masses of large, shiny seeds become a rich brown colour as they ripen. After seeding it can be cut down and within a few weeks will grow fresh foliage.

All parts of the plant are edible. The leaves can be added to salads and take the tartness from cooked fruit. The white, fibrous roots may be eaten raw or boiled. The ripe seeds were also traditionally ground to give a perfume to furniture polish.

Sweet cicely was once valued for medicinal purposes: the leaves as a sugar substitute for diabetics; for the treatment of coughs and flatulence; and as a gentle stimulant. One of the original 'pot' herbs, it was also used in healing ointments for ulcers and as a tonic or gentle laxative. It was a sovereign remedy in cases of stomach trouble. The roots of this plant are antiseptic.

Care

Sweet cicely needs rich, moist to moisture-retaining loam in order to thrive and a site in full sun, although it will tolerate partial shade.

New plants

Sow seeds in autumn (stratify); divide in spring.

H to 90cm (36in)
S to 60cm (24in)

18–20°C
(64–68°F)

Full sun or partial shade

Fennel flower
Nigella sativa

Fennel flower, or nutmeg flower, is a decorative annual herb closely related to *Nigella damascena* (love-in-a-mist), but bears paler blue to nearly white flowers. The blooms have a fascinating construction: the globular, horned seed pods are carried above the flowers. The herb is in no way related to fennel.

Fennel flower looks best when grown in a patch or drift, possibly in a rock garden or in an open border. In early spring the seedlings make a brilliant, light green carpet. It self-seeds profusely.

The Romans used the black seeds in cooking. The aromatic, nutmeg-scented seeds are valued today as a seasoning in curries and many other dishes, for spreading on bread or cakes, and as a substitute for pepper. The seeds also have some medicinal properties and were employed to treat indigestion. The dried seed heads are highly decorative.

Care
Fennel flower will grow happily in any well-drained soil. It requires an open and sunny site.

New plants
Sow seeds in situ in spring or autumn. Some protection should be given for autumn-sown varieties.

H to 45cm (18in)
S to 15cm (6in)

15–17°C
(59–62°F)

Full sun

Basil

Ocimum

Sweet basil was brought to Europe from India in the sixteenth century and has become one of the most popular culinary herbs. There are a number of varieties with different coloured leaves ranging from dark red to light green.

Sweet basil has a strongly aromatic, clove-like scent and is used extensively in the kitchen to season tomatoes, salads, vegetables, poultry and fish, and to make Italian pesto sauce. The leaves are best fresh, but may be dried or, better still, preserved in olive oil or as a frozen paste.

All varieties and species of basil are decorative, particularly those with purple or ruffled foliage, and they provide an attractive range of leaf and flower. Their distinctive scents are an added bonus. Many can be used as decorative edgings, especially the miniature Greek bush basil. Grow basil in small troughs or pots indoors, on the windowsill, or outside during the summer, either in the soil or in containers.

Care
Basil prefers rich, well-drained, moisture-retentive soil and a sunny, sheltered site.

New plants
Sow seeds at 13°C (55°F) in spring, or in situ in summer.

H to 60cm (24in)
S to 30cm (12in)

16–18°C
(61–64°F)

Full sun

Oregano
Origanum

A favourite perennial Mediterranean herb used to flavour stews and many pasta dishes, oregano is a bushy, rhizomatous plant that carries many flowers on upright stalks. These are most attractive to bees and insects, and emerge pinkish white from deep red bracts, although there are a number of naturally occurring colour variations.

The herbs mainly used for culinary purposes are: *Origanum onites* (often called pot marjoram), although it is not easy to obtain; *O. hirtum* (Greek marjoram or oregano), which has a fiery hot taste; *O. majorana* (sweet marjoram); and *O. vulgare* (wild marjoram or oregano).

Care
Oregano likes a nutrient-rich, well-drained to dry, calcareous soil and a site in full sun. Cut back the stems of oregano after flowering to leave an attractive leafy mound until the herb grows up again in the following spring.

New plants
Sow seeds in spring; take cuttings in early summer. This plant self-seeds.

Perilla
Perilla frutescens

This colourful annual is valued in bedding schemes for its lovely purple-bronze foliage. Perilla adds a splash of rich colour to any planting and is beautifully set off by some of the soft green and silver herbs. It can be used as a colourful edging in the formal garden and is invaluable in the potager. Plant it in bold groups to give dramatic colour and accent.

It is used extensively in Japan, where it is known as shiso: the cinnamon-scented leaves provide a flavouring; the green variety is popular for sushi and tempura; and the purple form is favoured for pickling, as it imparts its colour to the liquid. Use also in salads, soups and with vegetables. The leaves have an added hint of curry.

Care
Perilla prefers rich, moisture-retaining loam. It requires a site in partial shade.

New plants
Pre-chill seeds in moist sand at 5°C (41°F) for three days (leave seeds uncovered), then sow seeds in spring at 21–27°C (70–80°F).

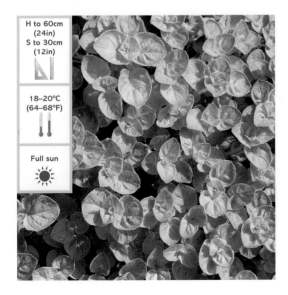

H to 60cm (24in)
S to 30cm (12in)

18–20°C (64–68°F)

Full sun

H to 60cm (24in)
S to 23cm (9in)

16–18°C (61–64°F)

Partial shade

Parsley

Petroselinum crispum

Parsley is a biennial often grown as an annual. It is one of the best-known herbs in the kitchen and is sprinkled over vegetables as a garnish, and added to soups and stews. Parsley sauce is a traditional accompaniment for fish dishes. Parsley is rich in vitamin C and is used in the treatment of urinary disorders. It makes an excellent edge in a container of herbs. There are a number of varieties available. The flat-leaved parsley, or French parsley, is hardier than the curly-leaved varieties and has a stronger flavour. *Petroselinum tuberosum* (turnip-rooted or Hamburg parsley), has a large root that can be cooked or eaten raw.

Care
Parsley grows best in fertile, moisture-retentive soil and on a site in full sun, although it will tolerate partial shade.

New plants
Sow seeds in summer. It is difficult to germinate and requires a high temperature. It helps to soak the seed in warm water overnight and pour boiling water down the seed drills. It needs to be sown in situ as it resents being disturbed.

H to 60cm (24in)
S to 60cm (24in)

18–20°C
(65–70°F)

Full sun or
partial shade

Rosemary
Rosmarinus officinalis

Rosemary has been used in the home since Roman times and old herbals tell of the many properties of the plant. It is the herb of remembrance and friendship, and is supposed to stimulate the mind. An evergreen shrub, it can be grown easily in any container herb garden given a sheltered position, for although it comes from the Mediterranean, it will tolerate some degree of frost. It flowers early in the year at the end of winter. In the kitchen it is the traditional accompaniment for roast lamb and can be used to flavour a number of other dishes. It is a slightly untidy plant, although some varieties are more compact than others, but it will not regenerate from old wood so care must be taken when trimming it back.

Rosemary is also extensively used in the cosmetics industry. Fresh or dried rosemary has some insect-repellent properties and is a natural antioxidant. Medicinally, rosemary has diverse properties and is valued especially for the treatment of headaches, poor circulation, digestion and as a hair tonic.

Care
Rosemary prefers well-drained, poor soil containing some lime. It likes a sheltered and sunny location.

New plants
Take semi-ripe cuttings or layer in summer.

H to 1.8m (6ft)
S to 90cm (36in)

16–18°C
(61–64°F)

Full sun

Common sage

Salvia officinalis

Salvias are a large group of plants, including annuals, biennials, perennials and shrubs, that are found in many gardens. Some are hardy, others that come from the tropics are greenhouse plants. The common sage, *Salvia officinalis*, and its varieties have been the best culinary herb for centuries and were formerly used in herbal medicine to treat depression, liver disorders, sore throats and mouth ulcers. An evergreen perennial or subshrub, the leaves are often dried and stored for use, and it is the main ingredient in sage and onion stuffing, a traditional accompaniment for roast poultry. It is also used to flavour fish, meat and cheese dishes.

Care

Sage prefers a well-drained, sandy loam and thrives in an open, sunny site. These herbs grow naturally in hot, dry, harsh conditions and must have good drainage if they are to survive hard, wet winters. They also require plenty of space and good air circulation to keep them dry at the base. Cut back the plants lightly after flowering and, if more drastic action is needed, cut back harder in spring.

New plants

Sow seeds in a cold frame in spring; take semi-ripe cuttings in summer.

H to 60cm (24in)
S to 60cm (24in)

18–20°C
(64–68°F)

Full sun

Salad burnet
Sanguisorba minor

This medieval 'pot' herb was much used in the kitchen to flavour soups, sauces and cheese, and its leaves were also eaten raw in salads. Medicinally, the leaves were dried and used as a tea to cure digestive disorders and to treat diarrhoea and haemorrhages. The roots, also used as a decoction for burns, make a black dye used in tanning. *P. sanguisorba* is a clump-forming perennial and if grown in a container has to be divided every two or three years to keep the plant within bounds. Herbaceous burnets, such as *S. canadensis* (Canadian burnet) and *S. officinalis* (greater burnet), have large bottlebrush flowers on terminal spikes.

Care
Salad burnet prefers poor, chalky soil and a sunny site.

New plants
Sow seeds in situ in spring; divide plants in spring.

Summer savory
Satureja hortensis

There are two sorts of savory. Winter savory is a foliage plant ideal for a low-growing container and often used to flavour beans. Summer savory is an annual, that can be grown to fill any bare areas. The hairy, erect stems have small white flowers on spikes in the summer. If they are grown for use in the kitchen, the plants should be pulled up and allowed to dry naturally, and then the leaves should be picked off and stored. The flavour is slightly reminiscent of thyme and the herb can be used sparingly in a number of meat dishes and stuffings. A tea made from the leaves acts as a tonic and flowering shoots will repel moths when used in clothes.

Care
Summer savory prefers well-drained, sandy loam. It requires an open, sunny site.

New plants
Sow seeds in situ in spring when the soil has warmed up.

H to 60cm (24in)
S to 60cm (24in)

15–17°C (60–62°F)

Full sun

H to 30cm (12in)
S to 30cm (12in)

15–17°C (59–62°F)

Full sun

Winter savory

Satureja montana

Winter savory has been used as a culinary herb since the ninth century, and is the perfect flavouring for beans. This is a decorative foliage plant, ideal for growing in the rock garden or on gravel. The more delicate, creeping variety will tumble over rocks and spread over gravel. As a native of mountain regions, it will survive cold winters only if it is given sharp drainage and rather poor soil.

Care

Winter savory likes well-drained to dry, alkaline or sandy loam and a site in full sun.

New plants

Surface-sow seeds in autumn (germination can be erratic); take semi-ripe cuttings in early summer.

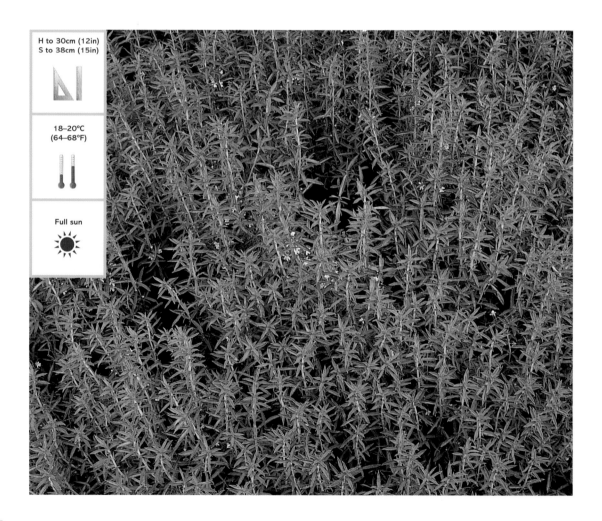

H to 30cm (12in)
S to 38cm (15in)

18–20°C
(64–68°F)

Full sun

Tansy

Tanacetum vulgare

Crisp or fern-leaved tansy, an old cottage-garden herb, is one of the best herbaceous foliage plants. Allow tansy to form clumps in the border or woodland edge. It withstands periods of drought and dislikes wet soils. Cut the plant down to the base when the leaves lose their freshness.

Tansy has long been valued as an insecticide; it was used as a strewing herb. It is valued medicinally for expelling intestinal worms and to treat scabies. In Britain tansy cakes and pudding were traditional at Easter.

The flowers and leaves yield yellow and green dyes for wool.

Care
Tansy prefers soil that is sharply drained and alkaline, and a site that is in full sun.

New plants
Divide in the autumn; take cuttings in the spring and summer; sow the seeds in spring.

H to 1.2m (4ft)
S to 90cm (36in)

18–20°C
(64–68°F)

Full sun

Common thyme

Thymus vulgaris

A well-known and important herb, common thyme is a perennial subshrub and is still used in the kitchen after many centuries in *bouquets garni* to flavour meat, fish and vegetable dishes. It is a charming, attractive plant for the herb container, and a 'lawn' composed of carpeting thymes of mixed colours and textures looks spectacular in bloom. Thymes will cascade over a low wall and if planted between paving slabs, they will spread and soften the edges.

There are a number of thymes that can be used in the kitchen, including *Thymus herba-barona*, with the scent of caraway, traditionally used to flavour a baron of beef, and some creeping thymes.

Care

Thymes thrive in extremely dry conditions, most preferring a gritty or gravelly soil in direct sunlight. Surround creeping thymes with a layer of sand, gravel or small stones placed on the soil's surface so that the mat of leaves is kept dry and clean. Lightly trim back bushy thymes after they have flowered.

New plants

The many creeping thyme varieties can be easily propagated by division. Most of the 'decorative' thymes do not produce seeds or do not come true from seeds.

H to 30cm (12in)
S to 30cm (12in)

16–18°C
(61–64°F)

Full sun

Heartsease
Viola tricolor

Heartsease, or Johnny-jump-up, is a delightful wild flower that blooms continuously all summer and well into the autumn. It readily cross-pollinates with other violas to produce a wide range of colour combinations. Hundreds of varieties of violas and violettas are available from specialised growers and suppliers. This is a lovely small flower for the container gardener, as it can be planted around the edges of the containers to provide long-lasting colour and interest.

Heartsease self-seeds everywhere. It will thrive in the rock garden, in gravelly or sandy areas, and in a border or even a formal herb garden. It enjoys hot sun.

Medicinally, it was used as a blood purifier, for fevers, as a gargle, and to treat ulcers and sores. It is fed to racing pigeons as a tonic and blood purifier. The dainty little blooms can be sprinkled on green salads.

Care
Heartsease grows best in fertile to sandy loam. It enjoys a site in full sun.

New plants
Sow seeds in spring in containers in a cold frame. Take tip cuttings in summer, if wanted. The plant self-seeds freely.

H to 30cm (12in)
S to 20cm (8in)

18–20°C
(64–68°F)

Full sun

Acanthus
Acanthus mollis

Sometimes known as bear's breeches, acanthus is a stately plant. Its tall spikes of mauve-and-white flowers make a stunning sight in summer, and the dark green, glossy, deeply divided leaves are highly decorative – in fact, they inspired ancient Greek architectural embellishment. The plant was also used medicinally by the ancient Greeks.

Acanthus is a specimen plant. Grow it so that the fine foliage and the magnificent flower spikes can be seen to best advantage. It looks wonderful in an island bed or border, where the surrounding plants should be much lower-growing.

In regions where acanthus will not survive the winter it can be grown successfully in a large container. In the first winter especially, it is necessary to give the plant a deep mulch, at least 15cm (6in), of leaves, bracken, straw or similar material to protect it from freezing temperatures.

Care
Acanthus likes well-drained, loamy soil and a site in full sun, although it will tolerate partial shade.

New plants
Sow seeds in spring; divide in autumn or spring; take root cuttings in winter.

H to 1.5m (5ft)
S to 50cm (20in)

15–17°C
(59–62°F)

Full sun or
partial shade

Yarrow
Achillea millefolium

Yarrow is an aromatic perennial. The attractive foliage is made up of thousands of tiny leaves (hence the name *millefolium*).

Since it seeds profusely, yarrow must be kept within bounds. Seed heads should be cut off before they ripen and at this stage can be hung up to dry, to be used in decorative dried arrangements. This plant is a good subject to naturalise in an area of wild grasses.

Yarrow was once used as a wound poultice in ancient times. Many of its common names refer to its ability to stem the flow of blood. It is also valuable as a remedy for fever and as a digestive tonic. A useful dye plant, it produces browns and greens.

Care
Yarrow prefers poor, well-drained soil. It is a good plant for chalky and seaside gardens. It prefers a site in full sun, although it will tolerate partial shade.

New plants
Sow seeds in spring; divide in spring or autumn; take softwood cuttings in early summer.

H to 60cm (24in)
S to 40cm (16in)

18–20°C
(64–68°F)

Full sun or
partial shade

Anise hyssop

Agastache foeniculum

This native of the North American prairies is a beautiful plant with anise-scented leaves and decorative spikes of mauve-purple flowers. It is often known as *Agastache anethiodora*, or blue giant hyssop.

Anise hyssop is an excellent flower for beekeepers since it attracts honeybees and bumblebees. It also looks stunning planted in a border or island bed with other herbs and wild plants. Unfortunately, anise hyssop is short-lived and it is best to take a few cuttings every year to ensure that it is not lost over the winter.

The fresh or dried leaves of the plant are used for flavouring and for tea. The dried flowers are a good ingredient for potpourri. The herb also has medicinal properties and a leaf tea is used for fevers, coughs and colds.

Care
This plant is happiest in well-drained loam situated in direct sunlight.

New plants
Sow the seeds in the spring.

H to 90cm (36in)
S to 60cm (24in)

15–17°C
(59–62°F)

Full sun

Bugle
Ajuga reptans

Bugle has shiny, dark green and purple, oval leaves and spikes of purple-blue flowers. It is a densely spreading plant that makes a superb ground cover. There are several extremely decorative forms, such as 'Atropurpurea' (beet-coloured leaves), 'Burgundy Glow' (magenta leaves edged with cream) and 'Variegata' (grey-green leaves edged with cream).

In the garden bugle requires a moist and humus-rich soil, and in hot regions some shade from the sun. It will grow well through gravel, provided there is good soil and some moisture underneath, and it thrives in a damp area near a pond, in a hedgerow, or in shade.

Bugle was traditionally known as the carpenter's herb, as it was used to stop bleeding.

Care
Bugle prefers humus-rich, moist to damp soil and a site in full sun, although it will tolerate partial shade.

New plants
Sow seeds in summer and autumn (germination can be erratic); plantlets produced by runners.

H to 30cm (12in)
S indefinite

15–17°C
(59–62°F)

Full sun or
partial shade

Lady's Mantle
Alchemilla vulgaris

Lady's mantle makes a dense ground cover. This attractive herb is often used to edge a border, especially to fall over hard paving. Trim the flower heads back after blooming; the plant will then continue to flower through the summer.

The species usually grown in gardens is *Alchemilla mollis*, from Asia Minor. It is vigorous and has hairy leaves that give it a softer look. There are also several low-growing alpine species, including *A. alpina*, which are excellent for the rock garden.

An important medicinal herb in the sixteenth century, lady's mantle is now used to treat menstrual and digestive disorders. The dried flower heads of all species look good in flower arrangements.

Care
Lady's mantle should be grown in a deep loam in order to thrive. It requires a site in full sun, although it will tolerate partial shade.

New plants
Sow seeds in spring to early summer; divide roots in spring or autumn; self-seeds.

H to 45cm (18in)
S to 60cm (24in)

18–20°C
(64–68°F)

Full sun

Marsh mallow
Althaea officinalis

As its name suggests, the beautiful herb marsh mallow, also known as mallard, grows in damp places. A tall, stately plant with an abundance of grey-green, soft, velvety leaves, it bears masses of delicate pink flowers in late summer. The seed heads resemble small, flat, round 'cheeses', in which each seed forms a segment.

The marsh mallow looks attractive growing near water or in clumps at the back of an island bed or border, where its muted foliage makes a backdrop for other, brighter flowers. It is an excellent feature plant, too.

Marsh mallow, in common with most other members of the mallow family, has since earliest times been used for food, and all parts of the plant are edible. The roots were once used to make the sweets known as marshmallows; they can also be cooked as a vegetable, and the young leaves and shoots may be eaten in salads.

Medicinally, this herb has been valued for its soothing properties to treat inflammation, coughs, bronchitis and hoarseness. Externally, the leaves are used as a poultice and to relieve the pain and swelling of bee stings.

Care
Marsh mallow prefers rich, moisture-retaining to damp soil. It thrives in salty seaside conditions and a site in full sun.

New plants
Sow seeds in spring (germination can be erratic); take cuttings in early summer; divide roots when dormant.

Hollyhock
Althaea rosea

The hollyhock was imported into Europe from China in the sixteenth century. It comes in a diverse range of flower colours, from white and the palest shades of yellow to rich reds, pinks and a deep purple-black. There are also double forms. It is a stately plant that looks good, and grows best, against a wall. Hollyhocks love good drainage and thrive in brick and lime rubble.

In suitable conditions hollyhock self-seeds readily. It is this random seeding that produces the groups of hollyhocks with flowers of different shades that are so appealing.

Hollyhock has similar medicinal properties to *Alathea officinalis*. The flowers are used as a tisane to treat chest complaints, or as a mouthwash.

Care
Hollyhocks need a well-drained soil in a site in full sunlight.

New plants
Sow seeds in spring or late summer; self-seeds.

Bearberry

Arctostaphylos uva-ursi

Bearberry is also commonly known by its Latin name of *uva-ursi*. This evergreen herb is an attractive ground-cover plant, with small, shiny, dark green leaves and tiny, pink-tipped, white flowers followed by red berries in the autumn. Bearberry grows best where there is no chalk in the soil and prefers acid conditions. If there are conifers in the garden, it will greatly enjoy the dappled shade beneath them where the tree litter is acidic.

This herb has important medicinal properties, which are particularly valued by herbal practitioners in the treatment of urinary, bladder and kidney infections,

but it should not be used for home treatment. The berries yield ash-grey and blue dye.

Care
Bearberry likes light, humus-rich, rather dry to sandy soil, with some moisture. It prefers a site in direct sunlight, although it will tolerate partial shade.

New plants
Sow seeds in the autumn; layer shoots, and take greenwood cuttings in summer.

H to 30cm (12in)
S to 60cm (24in)

15–17°C
(60–62°F)

Full sun or
partial shade

Arnica

Arnica montana

Also called mountain tobacco, arnica is a much valued perennial herb in medicine, and arnica ointment is used to treat bruises and sprains. It is also used in homeopathy to treat epilepsy, high blood pressure and shock. As with all medicinal herbs, it should not be used in its natural state as the plant is poisonous and toxic, and can cause skin irritation. It is not a large plant and carries attractive yellow flowers. It is a popular plant for growing in containers.

Care
Arnica prefers humus-rich, acid, sandy soil and an open, sunny site.

New plants
Sow fresh seeds in autumn or early spring; divide in spring.

H to 60cm (24in)
S to 15cm (6in)

16–18°C
(61–64°F)

Full sun

Red orache

Atriplex hortensis var. *rubra*

Red orache is an arresting herb with a deep red stem and purple-red leaves. A single plant in rich soil will grow to a substantial size with several stems and will make an impressive architectural feature plant if given space around it. It self-seeds profusely if allowed, and seedlings will appear the following spring. Orache is also available in golden-leaved and green-leaved forms, both of which are very decorative in the garden.

Orache is also known as mountain spinach, which indicates its culinary use. Young leaves may be added to salads, cooked like spinach, or made into a soup. For use as a vegetable, the plant must be given plenty of water when growing or the leaves will be tough. Medicinally, orache was used to treat sore throats and jaundice. At the end of the season, dry the seed heads for winter arrangements.

Care
This plant requires moisture-retaining, fertile loam and a site in full sun.

New plants
Sow seeds in late spring or autumn.

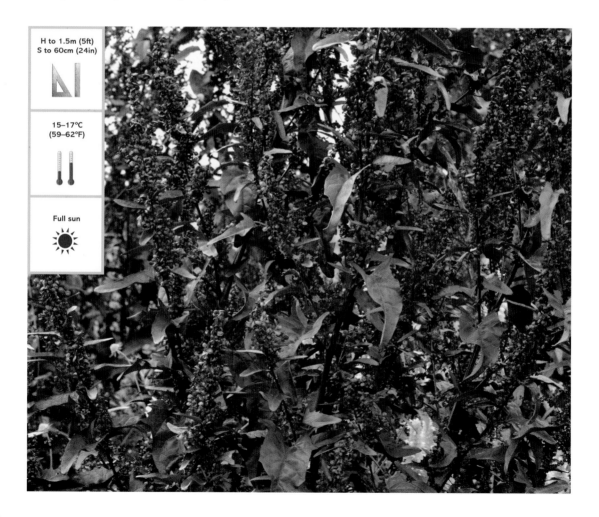

H to 1.5m (5ft)
S to 60cm (24in)

15–17°C
(59–62°F)

Full sun

Pot marigold

Calendula officinalis

Pot marigold is one of the most colourful of all perennial herbs and among the easiest to grow. The plant often seeds itself, but seeds can be sown in spring, and the plants will be in full flower during summer. Pot marigold really brightens up the herb garden and can be grown equally well in a flower border or an island bed. It looks much more natural grown as an individual plant rather than en masse. These plants used to be grown as a vegetable, but have fallen from favour as the leaves are rather bitter. Young leaves can be used in salads, and the flowers can be sprinkled on salads and soups as decoration. They can also be dried and used as a colouring or a substitute for saffron. Medicinally, pot marigold was used as an antiseptic and in the treatment of gangrene.

Care
Pot marigold will thrive in loam and most garden soils. This plant will tolerate dry conditions and prefers a site in full sun.

New plants
Sow seeds in situ in spring. Thin seedlings to 15cm (6in) apart.

H to 60cm (24in)
S to 45cm (18in)

18–20°C
(64–68°F)

Full sun

Feverfew

Chrysanthemum parthenium

Once known as flirtwort, this native of southeastern Europe has now spread far afield in gardens and naturalised in the wild over most of Europe and North America. Feverfew is a multi-branched plant; the masses of white, daisy-like flowers have yellow centres. The whole plant is strongly aromatic, and the leaves are bitter to taste.

In the garden feverfew looks its best in a large group and thrives in well-drained or even dry locations. It spreads extensively from seed if not cut down after flowering.

Feverfew has a long tradition as a medicinal herb to treat fevers and indigestion, and it is also a sedative. In recent years this herb, taken in tablet form or as fresh leaf, has assumed new importance in the treatment of migraine and arthritis, and is now a registered medicine in Britain, where it has been extensively researched. The dried leaves are also useful in the home as a moth-repellent.

Care
Feverfew prefers well-drained soil of any type. It requires a site in full sun, although it will tolerate partial shade.

New plants
Sow seeds in spring or late summer; self-seeds.

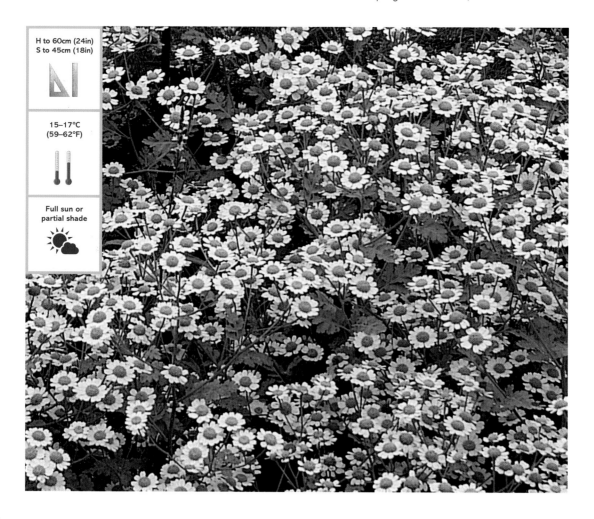

H to 60cm (24in)
S to 45cm (18in)

15–17°C
(59–62°F)

Full sun or
partial shade

Foxglove
Digitalis

The stately foxglove is one of our best-loved and most elegant wild flowers. It often occurs in large, dramatic stands in woodland clearings, sometimes in profusion on roadsides, and even on rocky hillsides.

This herb can be grown in a wide range of situations in the garden and is very adaptable, but it looks best in a fairly shady position, against a dark background created by trees or shrubs. Foxgloves always look stunning, whether planted in large stands or growing singly as graceful specimens. They produce tens of thousands of dust-like red-brown seeds and self-seed readily. If they are cut down after flowering to avoid seeding, they will sometimes live for another year.

The properties of foxglove leaves as a heart tonic were discovered in 1785, and the plant has played an important role in medicine ever since. Foxglove is, however, poisonous and should not be used except by qualified practitioners.

Care
Foxglove likes well-drained, moisture-retaining loam to light, sandy soil. It requires a site in partial shade or shade.

New plants
Sow seeds in late summer; self-seeds.

Warning This plant is poisonous.

H to 1.2m (4ft)
S to 30cm (12in)

18–20°C
(65–70°F)

Shade or
partial shade

Purple coneflower

Echinacea purpurea

This important perennial medicinal herb is native to North America, where the dried, powdered root was used by the Plains Indians as an antibiotic to cure rabies, snakebite and septicaemia. Today it is used in homeopathic medicine and is thought to have beneficial effects, boosting the immune system. With their petals radiating from a prominent centre, coneflowers are rather like giant daisies, to which family they belong. The name comes from the Greek word *echinops* ('hedgehog'), an allusion to the bristles on the bracts of the flowers.

Care
Purple coneflower prefers fertile, well-drained soil that retains some moisture in summer. It requires a site in full sun, although it will tolerate partial shade.

New plants
Sow seeds in late spring or early summer at 21°C (70°F); divide in spring or autumn.

H to 60cm (24in)
S to 23cm (9in)

16–18°C
(61–64°F)

Full sun or
partial shade

Joe-Pye weed

Eupatorium purpureum

Joe-Pye weed is a charming name for this spectacular, tall, North American plant, sometimes called queen of the meadow. However, Joe-Pye weed is not a meadowland plant; instead, it grows in open woods, scrub and at the water's edge, on moist soils, although it tolerates drier situations.

Joe-Pye weed is more impressive than its close relative, the European hemp agrimony. It looks its best at the rear of a border with shrubs and trees as a backdrop. Alternatively, it can be planted with dramatic effect in moist ground by a pond or stream. It is very attractive to bees and butterflies.

Traditionally, this herb, along with the spotted Joe Pye, was used by the Indians and later by the first settlers to treat fevers. Today it is used by qualified herbalists in the treatment of urinary stones, gout and rheumatism.

Care
Joe-Pye weed prefers a rich, moist, calcareous loam and a site in full sun, although it will tolerate partial shade.

New plants
Divide in spring or autumn; sow seeds in spring.

H to 2.7m (9ft)
S to 60cm (24in)

16–18°C
(61–64°F)

Full sun or
partial shade

Sweet woodruff
Galium odoratum

This herb is a woodland plant and should always be grown in the shade, as in bright sunlight the wonderful effect of the tiny, pure white flowers that are set against the decorative green foliage is lost. It is the perfect ground-cover plant, growing well among trees and shrubs, where it forms a dense, bright green carpet over the soil, suppressing most weeds. In good soil that is treated with leaf mould and has sufficient moisture, woodruff will romp away.

Woodruff seed is covered in tiny hooked bristles, which catch onto animal coats for wider distribution. The seed is difficult to germinate: it should be sown fresh in the autumn, and requires cold and frost to break its dormancy. It germinates in spring.

Sweet woodruff has been used since ancient times, particularly as a strewing herb. When dried, it smells wonderfully of new-mown hay, and it also has insect-repellent properties. As a medicinal herb, woodruff is a source of coumarin for anticoagulant drugs. A tea made from the plant relieves stomach ache, but is also a delicious drink.

Care
Plant sweet woodruff in humus-rich, moisture-retaining soil in shade.

New plants
Sow fresh seeds in late summer and divide after flowering.

H to 23cm (9in)
S to 20cm (8in)

18–20°C
(64–68°F)

Shade

Lady's bedstraw
Galium verum

The herb lady's bedstraw is also known as yellow bedstraw and cheese rennet, since it was once used for stuffing mattresses and also has the property of curdling milk.

This herb will thrive in poor, dry soil and is particularly at home near the sea. In certain areas of North America it has become a weed. Lady's bedstraw should be grown in a mass for the full dramatic effect of its tiny golden flowers and incredible honey scent. It is a good plant for clothing a dry bank or growing in poor ground, and can be mixed with suitable meadow grasses and other flowers of dry grassland to make a natural meadow.

A decoction of the dried flowers was used medicinally for urinary conditions and was once considered a treatment for epilepsy. The roots yield a lovely red dye similar to that produced by its relative, madder.

Care
This plant will do well in most well-drained soils. It requires a site in full sun, although it will tolerate partial shade.

New plants
Sow seeds or divide plants in autumn or spring.

Yellow gentian
Gentiana lutea

The spectacular yellow gentian produces many spires of brilliant yellow flowers with a hint of orange. It is not the easiest plant to grow and from seed will take at least three years to flower. When plants are raised, they should be transplanted young, since the yellow gentian puts down a long taproot, often several feet in length.

Plant the herb in the shady border in a small group. Provide it with a deep, alkaline soil that is well drained but still retains moisture. The taproot helps the plant to survive drought.

The long, thick root of yellow gentian is used to make tonic bitters for treating loss of appetite, and as a general tonic for the digestion. When seed has set, the dried stems of the plant make striking decorations.

Care
Yellow gentian prefers deep, well-drained but moisture-retaining loam. It requires a site in partial shade.

New plants
Sow seeds in autumn; divide mature crowns in spring.

H to 90cm (36in)
S to 40cm (16in)

15–17°C (59–62°F)

Full sun or partial shade

H to 1.8m (6ft)
S to 45cm (18in)

15–17°C (59–62°F)

Partial shade

Witch hazel
Hamamelis virginiana

Other names for this small tree are spotted alder, winterbloom and snapping hazelnut. The form of its growth is shrub-like, with several twisting stems coming from the base. It flowers in the depths of autumn and winter, after the leaves have fallen. Although each spider-like flower is quite small, a mature witch hazel in full bloom is highly decorative. The foliage turns a rich golden yellow in the autumn. Japanese and Chinese species are showier, with larger flowers.

Witch hazel will grow in partial shade, but in the garden it looks better in an open position, in full sun at the back of a border.

North American Indians used a decoction of witch hazel medicinally. Today its astringent properties are valued both medicinally and as additions to cosmetic preparations.

Care
Witch hazel likes moist, humus-rich soil, which is preferably neutral to acid. It requires a site in full sun, although it will tolerate partial shade.

New plants
Sow seeds in autumn; take softwood cuttings in summer.

Hop
Humulus lupulus

If you see a hop plant twining through a country hedge, you will notice that it is a very vigorous plant. Hop is easily grown from seeds but it is best to buy female plants. Their flowers are decorative and have the medicinal and flavouring properties, but they produce seed only if grown with the male plant. The large, dark leaves will quickly cover an old shed or climb a tall tree, and there will be a great display of cones to harvest.

Today the hop is employed as a safe and effective sedative – hence the use of hop pillows. The dried flower heads make attractive winter decorations. The strong, flexible vine is used in Scandinavia as a fibre to make cloth, and in basket making.

Care
Hops prefer humus-rich and moist or moisture-retaining soil that is well drained. It requires a site in full sun, although it will tolerate partial shade.

New plants
Sow seeds in autumn; take cuttings in early summer.

H to 4m (13ft)
S to 4m (13ft)

18–20°C (64–68°F)

Full sun or partial shade

H to 6m (20ft)
S to 6m (20ft)

16–18°C (61–64°F)

Full sun or partial shade

St John's wort
Hypericum perforatum

St John's wort is an attractive plant that can be grown in a border or against a wall, but looks its best among other wild plants in a natural area. In certain climates it can become a weed. St John's wort yields a profusion of tiny, brown, resin-scented seeds, which, in ideal conditions, produce thousands of seedlings.

This herb is the only member of the genus used medicinally, in both herbal and homeopathic medicine. The plant has vulnerary, sedative, antiviral, antidepressant, antibiotic and diuretic properties. Its leaves are used to treat wounds, bruises, burns and painful joints. The flowers yield a dye that turns silk and wool a violet-red but will not dye cotton.

Care
St John's wort grows well in most well-drained soils. It likes a site in full sun, although it will tolerate partial shade.

New plants
Sow seeds in autumn or spring; divide plants in the autumn.

H to 90cm (36in)
S to 30cm (12in)

18–20°C (64–68°F)

Full sun or partial shade

Elecampane
Inula helenium

Elecampane is a stately, impressive plant grown for its ample foliage as well as its sunflower-like blooms. This herb will provide structure and architectural focus to a planting, so give it plenty of space. In winter it disappears completely.

The plant seeds profusely. Cut the heads before the seeds are ripe or it could become a nuisance. The seed heads are beautifully marked once the seed has been cleaned out, and make good dried winter decorations.

Elecampane has been used as a medicinal herb since ancient times. The plant is a bactericide and tonic. The dried root is valued in the treatment of respiratory disorders. Elecampane is still used in the manufacture of some wines and liqueurs. The flowers yield a yellow dye and the roots give a blue.

Care
Elecampane is suited to any fertile, moisture-retaining soil. It requires a site in full sun to partial shade.

New plants
Sow seeds in spring or when ripe; divide rootstocks in the autumn.

H to 2m (6.5ft)
S to 90cm (36in)

16–18°C
(61–64°F)

Full sun or
partial shade

Great lobelia

Lobelia syphilitica

Great lobelia is often used as a medicinal substitute for *Lobelia inflata* (Indian tobacco), an annual of no great decorative value. Great lobelia, on the other hand, is a handsome and colourful plant, and is useful in the garden because it flowers so late – at the summer's end, when flowering plants are becoming scarce. It can be grown in any good soil that retains moisture, but in its natural habitat it is associated with water. Grow it in the bog garden or near the edge of a pond, where its roots will search out moisture throughout the summer. In a large clump it will give welcome colour when other waterside flowers have stopped blooming.

As its Latin name indicates, this was a herb that the Iroquois Indians employed to treat venereal disease: they made the root into a tea. Leaf tea was also employed for colds, fevers and stomach trouble.

Care
Great lobelia grows best in rich, moist or moisture-retaining soil. It requires a site in full sun.

New plants
Sow seeds in spring; surface-sow.

Purple loosestrife

Lythrum salicaria

Purple, or spiked, loosestrife is a handsome waterside plant for the pond, though in warm climates it can be invasive. In parts of North America it has taken over, and should always be introduced with caution.

The long purple flower stems look stunning beside water and produce thousands of tiny red-brown dust-like seeds. This plant should always be encouraged to form a good stand.

Purple loosestrife is still valued in herbal medicine; it has tonic, antibacterial and hemostatic properties. The plant rapidly stops bleeding, is a good wound cleanser, and makes an effective gargle.

Care
Purple loosestrife prefers a fertile, moist or wet soil. It should be planted in a site in full sun, although it will tolerate partial shade.

New plants
Sow seeds or divide in spring.

H to 90cm (36in)
S to 45cm (18in)

15–17°C (59–62°F)

Full sun

H to 1.2m (4ft)
S to 50cm (2in)

16–18°C (61–64°F)

Full sun or partial shade

Horehound

Marrubium vulgare

Useful in the herb garden for its distinctive texture and colour, horehound's soft, silvery green foliage and 'frosted' appearance have a subtle charm. It is an undemanding plant to grow and prefers the poorest conditions. Take advantage of its drought-resistant qualities.

Horehound is a useful foliage plant that blends well with a wide range of herbs and makes an attractive foil for brighter-coloured flowers.

In England horehound beer was formerly very popular and sweets were made from the juice of the plant. Medicinally, the herb's greatest value is in the treatment of bronchitis, coughs and sore throats, and as a bitter digestive tonic.

Care
Horehound needs well-drained, sandy, dry and poor soil in order to thrive, on a site in full sunlight.

New plants
Take cuttings in summer; divide roots in spring; stratify seeds and sow in spring or autumn. Germination can be erratic.

H to 90cm (36in)
S to 45cm (18in)

15–17°C
(59–62°F)

Full sun

Peppermint

Mentha × piperita

Peppermint is used in flavouring, and also in cosmetics and soaps. It is quite a large perennial and reaches 90cm (36in) in height. It can be planted in containers where its red stems and crisp, red-tinted leaves look attractive. It is the most valuable of all the mints medicinally. Fields of peppermint are grown commercially, and the essential oils distilled for a number of uses. In England the centre of the peppermint industry used to be the town of Mitcham in Surrey. The plant is a hybrid of *Mentha aquatica* (watermint), and *M. arvensis* (cornmint).

Care

Peppermint needs well-drained, fertile, moisture-retentive soil and an open, sunny site. It needs to be contained and the traditional way of doing this in the garden was to plant them in an old bucket with the bottom removed sunk into the soil.

New plants

Divide runners in autumn. Never attempt to grow any mint from seed as the varieties are unlikely to breed true.

Warning Mints have hairy leaves that can cause skin irritations and rashes. Handle them with care. Similarly, mint tea should not be drunk continuously over a long period.

H to 90cm (36in)
S to 45cm (18in)

16–18°C
(61–64°F)

Full sun

Bergamot
Monarda

Wild bergamot enjoys being in dryish soils but is a woodland-edge plant, so give it some shade from the hottest midday sun and grow it in a situation where trees, shrubs or a hedge form a background feature. For a striking effect, plant wild bergamot in a good-sized clump. Grow it with other drought-tolerant herbs that enjoy light shade, such as *Galium verum* (lady's bedstraw), *Origanum vulgare* (wild marjoram) and the popular *Digitalis grandiflora* (yellow foxglove).

Monardas can easily be propagated by 6–10cm (2½–4in) tip cuttings taken from late spring to late summer. The roots of mature plants can also be divided into smaller sections to make new plants. Try to divide them every two or three years.

Care
Monarda likes to be planted in well-drained, dryish loam or sandy soil in partial shade, although it will tolerate full sun for most of the time.

New plants
Sow seeds in the spring; take cuttings from late spring to late summer; divide plants in the autumn or spring.

H to 90cm (36in)
S to 45cm (18in)

16–18°C
(61–64°F)

Partial
shade

Evening primrose
Oenothera biennis

Evening primrose is something of a misnomer as, although many species open their flowers at dusk, they are often open for much of the day, especially in cloudy weather. Their wonderful, intense fragrance is most noticeable at night. The tall *Oenothera biennis* is most suited to any dry situation or stony ground, where a selection of evening primroses can be grown.

Evening primrose has recently become an important medicinal herb used to treat premenstrual syndrome, multiple sclerosis and other conditions. The thick root of the plant has been used as a vegetable.

Care
Evening primrose prefers well-drained soil and a site in full sunlight.

New plants
Sow seeds in late summer; self-seeds.

H to 1.2m (4ft)
S to 45cm (18in)

18–20°C
(64–68°F)

Full sun

Rue

Ruta graveolens

Rue, once called the herb of grace, has long been used medicinally. It is a decorative garden plant, particularly the variety 'Jackman's Blue', which has more ample, blue-green foliage and blends especially well with silver and grey herbs.

It will grow on the poorest, driest of soils, and although it will do well in rich, fertile soil, it will be less hardy. It enjoys a hot, sunny site in the bed or border and also thrives in gravel.

Rue has long been regarded as an excellent antiflea herb. In homeopathic medicine it is used as an ointment for sprains and strains. It is too powerful to use as a home remedy.

Care
Rue needs well-drained, calcareous and not too fertile soil, and a site in full sunlight.

New plants
Sow seeds in spring; take cuttings in early summer.

Warning Rue can cause a phototoxic rash. Wear gloves when handling, especially in sunlight.

Skullcap

Scutellaria lateriflora

Skullcaps grow all over the world, although the majority are native to North America. The plant is known as mad-dog skullcap in the USA, where it was considered a treatment for rabies. The name skullcap comes from the miniature seed capsule, which opens like a helmet when the seed is ripe and ready for dispersal.

The mad-dog skullcap is a modest plant whose main use in the garden is as ground cover in moist, shady areas among trees and shrubs. It spreads rapidly in damp soils by pale yellow underground runners. There are many other species, some of which are well worth growing in the garden.

The plant is now considered an effective medicinal for the treatment of the nervous system, on which it acts as a tonic.

Care
Skullcap prefers moist to moisture-retaining, fertile loam. It requires a site in shade, although it will tolerate partial shade.

New plants
Sow seeds or divide plants in spring.

H to 90cm (36in)
S to 45cm (18in)
15–17°C (59–62°F)
Full sun

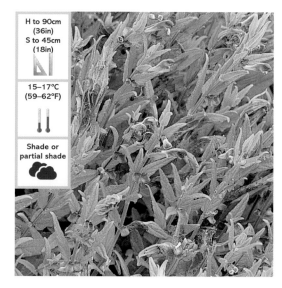

H to 90cm (36in)
S to 45cm (18in)
15–17°C (59–62°F)
Shade or partial shade

Russian comfrey

Symphytum × uplandicum

Grow Russian comfrey in a plot of its own for use in composting. Well-manured, it can be cut down up to six times a season. Other species also make attractive garden plants: *Symphytum grandiflorum*, with creamy pink flowers, produces excellent ground cover; *S. peregrinum* has intense blue flowers; and *S. orientale* bears cream-coloured blooms.

Comfrey, also known as knitbone, boneset and bruisewort, is an old and valuable medicinal plant. A leaf poultice is used externally for bruises, burns, wounds and ulcers, and a leaf tea given for gastric ulcers, pleurisy and bronchitis.

Care
Russian comfrey likes rich, moisture-retaining loam. It needs a site in full sunlight, although it will tolerate partial shade.

New plants
Sow seeds in summer or autumn; divide roots in spring.

Warning This plant is phototoxic.

H to 1.2m (4ft)
S 90cm (36in)

18–20°C
(64–68°F)

Full sun or
partial shade

Valerian
Valeriana officinalis

Valerian, also known as all-heal, is an old medicinal plant whose use dates back to the tenth century.

It is very ornamental, with masses of frothy pink flowers and attractive foliage, and looks its best planted near water, alongside other herbs from a similar habitat. Valerian will spread and form a large clump in time. It self-seeds to a limited extent.

Medicinally, valerian is used as a herbal tranquilliser to treat insomnia, hypertension, nervous exhaustion and anxiety. Herbal preparations that contain valerian are widely favoured in Europe. In the USA, however, this natural medicine is prohibited.

Care
Valerian prefers fertile, moist to moisture-retaining loam. It should be situated in direct sunlight, although it will tolerate partial shade.

New plants
Sow seeds in spring; divide roots in spring or autumn.

H to 1.5m (5ft)
S to 90cm (36in)

16–18°C
(61–64°F)

Full sun

Vervain
Verbena officinalis

Considered a sacred herb by the Romans, vervain was used to purify homes and temples, and was traditionally employed as a cure for dropsy. In England it is commonly found growing by roadsides and in sunny pastures.

The aerial parts of the plant are used as an effective nerve tonic, liver stimulant, urinary cleanser and fever remedy. They are also traditionally used to promote milk flow and can be taken during labour to encourage contractions.

Vervain has a number of topical uses, including on sores, wounds and gum disorders. It is also used to encourage sweating and to stimulate the immune system in feverish conditions.

Care
Vervain prefers fertile, moist to moisture-retaining loam. It should be situated in direct sunlight, although it will tolerate partial shade.

New plants
Sow seeds in spring; divide roots in spring or autumn.

Teasel
Dipsacus fullonum

The teasel is a tall and imposing plant with distinctive, spiny flower heads, which bloom in a unique way. The flowers form a band around the head, spreading up it, at no time covering it completely. The flowers are attractive to insects, particularly bees. The light green leaves form a deep cup, which fills with dew and rainwater.

Teasel should be seeded on waste ground by a stream or on a bare bank or other empty area. It will seed itself profusely if allowed.

Fuller's teasel (*Dipsacus fullonum* subsp. *fullonum*) is famous for its use in the cloth industry. The heads of this plant have bristly, hooked spines – unlike those of the common teasel – and once matured and dried, these were used to tease, or raise, the nap on woollen cloth. It is a cultivated sub-species that is well worth growing for interest. Collect all teasel seed heads when they are golden, before they are rained upon, to preserve their beautiful colour for winter decorations.

Care
Teasel likes moisture-retaining loam or clay and a site in full sunlight, although it will tolerate partial shade.

New plants
Sow seeds in late summer; self-seeds.

H to 90cm (36in)
S to 45cm (18in)

16–18°C (61–64°F)

Full sun or partial shade

H to 1.8m (6ft)
S to 45cm (18in)

15–17°C (59–62°F)

Full sun or partial shade

Catmint

Nepeta mussinii

There are many catmints suitable for the herb garden. They make lovely soft edging plants, with masses of summer blooms. Catmint will flower again in the autumn if cut back after the first long flowering.

This plant looks best when it is tumbling over the edge of a path or low wall, and is suitable for planting in an open border or a rock garden. The soft, grey-green foliage is a wonderful foil for brighter flowers.

Nepeta cataria (catnip) is the traditional herbal catmint. It grows tall and bears white flowers dotted with purple, and strongly scented, nettle-like leaves. Cats love this herb.

Catmint was traditionally a medicinal plant and is also used for tea.

Care
Catmint performs best in sandy or well-drained loam that is moist to dry. It requires a site in full sunlight, although it will tolerate partial shade.

New plants
Sow seeds or divide plants in spring; take cuttings in early summer.

Jacob's ladder

Polemonium caeruleum

Jacob's ladder is so called because of the ladder-like formation of its bright green leaves. This is a cottage flower that has been grown for many centuries in country gardens.

In times past the herb was used to treat fevers, headaches, epilepsy and nervous complaints.

Care
Jacob's ladder prefers humus-rich, moist to moisture-retaining, calcareous loam. It requires a site in full sunlight, although it will tolerate partial shade. It associates well with water, and with trees and shrubs. For a long flowering, cut down the stems before they go to seed. One stem will be more than adequate for self-seeding, since seeds are produced in abundance.

New plants
Sow seeds in spring or autumn; divide roots in spring; self-seeds.

H to 60cm (24in)
S to 45cm (18in)

16–18°C (61–64°F)

Full sun

H to 90cm (36in)
S to 30cm (12in)

18–20°C (64–68°F)

Full sun

Glossary

Annual A plant that completes its cycle of germination from setting seed through to dying in a single growing season.

Biennial A plant requiring two growing seasons to flower and seed.
Bract A leaf at base of flower stalk or flower head.
Bulb A plant storage organ, usually formed underground, containing the following year's growth buds.

Calyx Usually green, outer part of a flower, formed from the sepals, that encases the petals in bud.
Corm A swollen stem base that acts as a storage organ, similar to a bulb.
Crown The part of a herbaceous plant from where new stems are produced.
Cultivar A man-made or cultivated variety, produced by hybridisation.
Cutting A section of a plant removed for propagation.

Division The splitting of a plant clump into various sections containing roots and shoots; normally done when the plant is dormant, for purposes of propagating or reinvigorating the plant.
Double flowers Applied to a flower head or bloom having more petals than the original species.

Floret One of the individual flowers that make up the head of a composite flower, such as a dahlia.
Flower head A mass of small flowers that appear as one flower.
Force (-ing) A method of promoting early flowering or fruiting, usually via artificial heat and light.

Half-hardy A plant that withstands low temperatures but not freezing.
Hardy A plant that tolerates year-round conditions in temperate climates, including normal frost, without protection.
Herbaceous A non-woody plant that dies down to its rootstock in winter.

Hybrid A plant resulting from crossing two different species.

Inflorescence A group or arrangement of flowers on a stem, such as panicles and racemes.

Layering A method of pinning a stem to the ground and inducing it to form roots, thereby propagating a separate plant.

Mulch A layer of organic or inorganic material added to the surface of the soil to retain moisture, help suppress weeds and gradually improve fertility.

Node The point at which a leaf grows from the stem.

Offset A plant that is reproduced naturally from the base of the parent plant.

Perennial A plant that lives for longer than two seasons.

Raceme A long, unbranched flower stem.
Rhizome An underground, often creeping, stem acting as a storage organ, from which roots and shoots grow.
Rootball The roots together with the soil adhering to them when a plant is lifted, e.g., for transplanting.

Sepals The green outer parts of a flower, collectively forming the calyx.
Single flowers Applied to a flower that has the normal number of petals for its species, such as a daisy.

Type Used to refer to an original plant species.

Variety A variant of a plant species, arising either naturally or as a result of selection.

Index